THE UNC

The Unclear Path
Life Beyond Disability

Elizabeth Greeley

Hodder & Stoughton
LONDON SYDNEY AUCKLAND

British Library Cataloguing in Publication Data
A record for this book is available from the British Library

ISBN 0 340 66508 4

Printed and bound in Great Britain by
Cox & Wyman, Reading, Berkshire

Hodder and Stoughton Ltd
A Division of Hodder Headline PLC
338 Euston Road
London NW1 3BH

I dedicate this book to my beloved parents who have made many sacrifices on my behalf and given me freedom to be myself against all odds; to Kate, my speech therapist, for her endless support over the years with voice and physical problems, and her encouragement in other activities I have embarked on; and last but not least to Patrick Purnell SJ, to whom I am indebted for his love in helping me see that God is with me as I strive and struggle through life to follow him and to help others in whatever way I can.

A word of thanks is due to the many people who have helped me with typing and correcting the manuscript, and particularly to Joan Harding who helped me in the final stages of the book.

Contents

Foreword

The key into Liz's life is to know, in spite of the severest disability, what a loving God means. Of the man born blind in John's Gospel (John 9), Jesus says, 'Neither this man nor his parents sinned; he was born blind so that God's works might be revealed in him.' This is a staggering answer; it undermines our conventional understanding of God's goodness. God's work is revealed in and through the man born blind; and in a similar way God is revealed in and through the life of Liz. Liz discovered a God who suffers with her in her suffering so that she might find life, life in its fullness.

There are two constant themes in Liz's life. The first is to help other people. Her second theme is pain: 'Pain is an everyday occurrence', she writes almost prosaically. Helping other people is the driving force which enables Liz to bear pain and has made Liz free herself from depending on other people as much as she can in order to live as independently as possible. She lives alone in her own flat, relying on what services she needs coming to her doorstep. Her lifestyle is almost an act of defiance against all odds, as readers will perceive as they pursue the accumulated details of her disability.

Liz does not spare us the intimate details of her sufferings and the humiliations attendant on them but, as hard as it is for the reader to pursue this account, there is, nevertheless, nothing morbid about it, nor is there any element of self-pity.

This does not mean that Liz has not rebelled against her condition, and demanded of God the 'Why?' of her plight. She has had to fight depression and the loneliness of her almost unique predicament. Many other people have the particular form of cerebral palsy which makes Liz an athetoid. However, few of the doctors who have attended her have had previous experience of patients with the increasing problems that she has encountered. Liz has had to explain aspects of her condition to the doctors over and over again. She has had the constant problem of making people hear and understand what she says. Again and again she is asked to repeat what she says. She is mortified when people conclude she is drunk from the way she walks. Problems in ordinary actions, like swallowing, cause her an incredible intensity of pain. 'I hate the tube!' she says, referring to the way she has to feed herself. All of this has led her in the past to contemplate suicide. But 'Of course, I would never do it. It would hurt too many people.'

Liz writes a powerful story about herself, her God and her friends, but for all its power there is a sense in which it is something very mundane. There are the very ordinary relations with members of her family, except, perhaps, for one – her beloved brother, Vincent, who had hydrocephalus, 'which means that Vincent was born with too much fluid on the brain which made him have a large head'. She remembers the last service she did for him was to find a teaspoon with which he could be fed. There is Graham who falls in love with her. She does not reciprocate, and she describes the difficulty of distancing herself from him without hurting his feelings. There is the joy and fun of being responsible for a charity shop, which also sells antiques, watching that the customers do not steal anything. There is the excitement of living in a hostel and trying to do one's bit for the other residents. There are friends; the goodness in them cannot necessarily be strictly defined, but the hand of God has touched Liz through them. There is listening and listening to parents of handicapped children, to friends who drop in to tell their troubles, to neighbours and to anyone who needs a patient ear.

And in the midst of all this is God . . . Somehow Liz wanted to dedicate her life to God. Life as a member of a religious order was not for her. It became clear to her that God wanted some sort of commitment to prayer, celibacy and poverty, but not to obedience! This was because nearly all her life Liz had been told what to do. And so she dedicated herself to serve her fellow disabled in whatever way she could. This book is a part of achieving that ambition.

Patrick Purnell SJ

Introduction

For a number of years a few people have asked me to write my life story. For a long time I have had mixed feelings about this but as encouragement continued I began to question whether my story might help other people. Before I could answer that I had to look at my life and ask myself what kind of life I have had. The answer to this is that my life has been full of challenges, struggles, frustrations, increasing physical problems, excitement, fighting against the system and proving that inside a disabled body I am a person who can take responsibility for myself, who needs support from other people and has normal emotional feelings.

I then asked myself what has helped me get through life and there are a number of factors. My relationship with God is very important to me and plays a large part in my life. Somehow my faith helps me to see life as worth living against all the odds. In fact, it is my faith that has got me through. My relationship with God is much more than just fulfilling an obligation by going to Mass on a Sunday. Like other people I have my own prayer life outside the four walls of the church. The other major factor has been people. Their love, honesty, understanding, patience and humour have been invaluable to me. Just as important I have found and continue to find God in the goodness of the people I meet as I go about my everyday life. The people I meet may or may not be aware that I am experiencing the goodness of God from them.

Throughout my life I have had to struggle physically to learn how to do simple things that most people take for granted. But this is exciting once I am able to do something like doing up my shoelaces. I have overcome a barrier and I am more independent.

Sometimes, if I can't do something one way I have to think of how I can get round it. This is what it is like for a number of disabled people – a tussle with ingenuity. I have had to struggle over the years to accept my own disability, to be accepted as an equal like everyone else, to teach people by the way I live that being disabled is not the end of the world and that life is worth living.

Another thought that came to mind was that I only wanted to write my story if it was going to be of help to other people. Therefore, at the end of each chapter I have deliberately added a 'Reflection' in an attempt to show how some barriers concerning disability can be overcome. When I have written about major physical problems I have dealt with one disability in its own chapter in the hope that readers will then have a clearer understanding of how the people involved as well as myself tackle the problems. Attitudes toward, and facilities for, people who are born disabled have changed greatly since I was a child, and I have tried to compare things as they were then with the situation today.

I mentioned my faith but I am not only trying to help people who share my beliefs. I think the 1988 Vatican document – *Cristifideles Laiici*, concerning the role of the laity in the Roman Catholic Church – sums this up very well in the statement that disabled people are not only to be served but are responsible partners in the Church's mission and, I would add, in society. This is not always easy for people who are not disabled to accept; they may have difficulty in accepting their disabled sisters and brothers as co-partners. I hope that my insights will help.

I have tried to see the positive and negative elements of the different aspects of my life. I sincerely hope that what I write will encourage disabled people, their families and their friends to know that where there is love and compassion there is hope. I am not going to pretend that life has not been a struggle at times. Why should I, as in this day and age everybody has to struggle? But what I can do is to look back and see that God was with me in my struggle, just as God is with everyone else. Most of us can only see this when we look back rather than at the time.

Now I leave it to my readers to decide – has my life been exciting and full of challenge?

1

Childhood Days

Early Days

My parents were married in 1938 and at that time lived in Yorkshire. My mother was born in Escombe and grew up in Bishop Auckland in Durham. My father was a Yorkshireman and worked in an office. Then came the war. He was away for five years, part of which he spent in the Middle East. Before the war my mother worked as a clerk, but when the war started my brother Paul came along so she had to give up work to look after him. However, she did take in evacuees.

Soon after the war I was born, in the Royal Infirmary, Huddersfield, on 27th October 1946. There and then I was baptised Elizabeth Mary by one of the nurses on the ward because I was in danger of death. Later there was a family christening in which all the members of the family joined.

My life started with people thinking I may not pull through because I was born with cerebral palsy. This was caused by a lack of oxygen at the time of my birth. The form of cerebral palsy which I have makes me an 'athetoid'. Not many people know what athetoid means. I will explain it in my own words, which may not say what the medical books say but I am living with the problem every day of my life. Being athetoid means that I have a lot of involuntary movements. Because of my physical condition I had to work twice as hard at learning to do the ordinary, very simple things in life that able-bodied people usually take for granted and do without having to think. For example, I can be sitting still but if the telephone rings I will jump, and if I have a cup of tea in my hand at the time this generally gets spilt, usually over me!

When I walk, people who do not know me may think I'm drunk. They do not understand that one of my problems is that I lean over backwards and can't pick up my feet as other people can. I also have a speech defect and not everyone can understand me. Sometimes people become frightened, so I have to educate them to feel at ease not just for my sake, but for others who are in the same position. It is hard for me to feed myself and I often make a mess. It may look as though I don't care about the mess and my appearance, which gives people the wrong impression, but I am very conscious of it and do care about this. It is a constant struggle which I face every day of my life. These are just a few examples of what it feels like to be me.

Let me return to my early childhood. On his return from the war, my father went to Lancaster to train as a teacher. Later he took a degree in music. At this stage of my life I can't remember much about my father except for him saying that when I was born I looked blue. This would have been due to shortage of oxygen. My father's parents had died when he was still in his teens. My grandmother on my mother's side of the family lived nearby, which enabled my mother to visit her most days. Before the war she, Gran as we called her, ran a boys' club and during the war she was an air-raid warden. Her last job was cleaning for a panel of doctors. I can still remember her having a fag constantly hanging from her mouth. My grandfather had died before I was born.

There were eight children in the family. Paul was the eldest, then there was a seven-year gap because of the war and I came next. Clare and Ursula followed and then Vincent, who was also disabled. All of us were born in Yorkshire. By the time Martin, Mary and Felicity were born we had moved to Bexleyheath in Kent. They are all married now and, with the exception of Martin and Felicity, all have their own children. Martin has been married twice and his second wife has two children by her previous marriage. Felicity has adopted two children. So I have sixteen nephews and nieces. Vincent died, but that is a special story and I'll tell that later.

One of the things my parents did was to be involved in forming the local Spastics Society in Huddersfield. In those days people who had cerebral palsy were known as 'spastic'. That is how the society got its name. It has now been renamed 'Scope'. Obviously, I was too young to be aware of this but it is nice to know that my parents began to take action straight away in order to help me. At that time it seemed that parents in different parts of the country would form local groups to give each other support. It was round about the early fifties that the national Spastics Society (now called Scope) was founded and these local groups were given more help.

Like most people I do not remember much about my early childhood. My parents did not live far from my grandmother. Paul used to push me and my two sisters up to Gran's house. I remember it was a green pushchair. One of my earliest memories is of myself sitting in a playpen and watching Gran doing the washing in a tub, scrubbing the clothes and pulling them up and down to get everything clean.

My mother had to trail my two sisters, Clare and Ursula, along with me to the hospital three times a week so that I could have physiotherapy. This I cannot remember. She must have had her hands full! This care for me played a large part in family life at that time.

St Vincent's Hospital, Pinner

My first clear memory of my parents is when they took me to live at St Vincent's Orthopaedic Hospital in Pinner, run by the Sisters of Charity of St Vincent de Paul, so that I could have the best care and medical attention and a certain amount of schooling. I was considered far too disabled to go to school with able-bodied children. In those days, education was not a priority for children in residential hospitals. It was 1950 and I was four years old.

My parents were anxious that I should go to a place where I could have a Catholic upbringing. I can remember them leaving me in the care of Sister Joseph who was to become my lifelong friend. At St Vincent's I met other young children who, like me, had to leave their parents because of their disability. Sister Jo, as we called her, did her best to make our surroundings as homely as possible.

I stayed at St Vincent's for five years. At the beginning my parents could only come down from Huddersfield to visit me once a month. My mother would faithfully send me a letter and a parcel of chocolate sweets which would arrive on a Wednesday. I could not think of anything else until I had received this letter, so Wednesdays became a very special day for me.

At one time I had German measles and I was in quarantine for three weeks. Mother sent me some cards from the back of a cereal packet. The Wednesday letter would be full of news about members of my family.

In 1952, my parents decided to move. It didn't take my father long to find a job as a teacher in Kent. Schools were found for my brother Paul and my two sisters. This then enabled me to see more of the other members of my family.

On one occasion Martin came to see me with Father and all he wanted to do was play with Father's pen. Another time when Father came down on his own he was very worried about Vincent but he was able to talk to Sister Joseph about the problem. Looking back, I can now appreciate the great sacrifice my parents made so they could live near the hospital in order to see me more.

When I was learning to walk in the gym, I would walk between two physiotherapists who would stand on either side of me in case I lost my balance and fell. I could take a few steps on my own when I left home but I was very unsafe on my feet. To start with it had felt safer to crawl. I had a friend, Carol, who also had cerebral palsy and we used to crawl around the ward and mess up the sheets in order to put my teddy to bed. I am sure we drove the nurses mad. When I left St Vincent's I was not allowed to take my teddy with me because it was considered that he may be carrying some infection. I was more upset about having to leave my teddy behind than the fact that I was leaving St Vincent's. Slowly I grew in confidence and struggled to walk; even though I felt I might fall, which I often did.

When I was at Pinner we used to play a game where we would pretend we were different people. There was Ann, Carol, Carol Getgood, Marion and a few more whose names I can't remember. However, if you had a quarrel with someone you were out of the game and you had to win somebody's favour before you could be admitted back into the game. This game went on for about six months!

Towards the end of my stay at Pinner, my father would take me to the teashop when he came to visit. I can remember one day having had cake and lemonade and he said, 'Well done!' – I had not made too much of a mess. Improvement!

I was given a calliper to help my left foot grow straighter.

To this day I am convinced that this is what made my left foot become more shaky. Later, when I went to school, I was given walking sticks to start with but very soon they were taken away from me in case I damaged other people by poking an eye out (by accident of course!).

I made my first confession at about seven years old, as was customary for Catholic children. I made it to the hospital chaplain, Father Daly. Sister Kelly prepared me. She frightened the living daylights out of me because she was so stern. It was her job on Saturday night to come round and say night prayers in the children's ward. God help you if you had not got yourself covered up to the neck. She would tell you off for being immodest!

The same year I made my first communion. When Mother came to see me she would teach me 'Jesus, Thou Art Coming' and a hymn to my guardian angel. On the day of my first communion, my mother came up from Kent early so that she could be with me on this great day. I was in a wheelchair and had a kidney dish and towel behind my back in case I choked.

One incident has stayed in my mind from when I was eight or nine. The ice cream van came to the ward and like every other kid I wanted an ice cream. Ice cream was two pence but I had no money. However, I knew my father was coming and that he would give me the money. Therefore, I thought it would be OK to take two pence from Sister's desk because when Father came I could put it back. This is what I proceeded to do and did I enjoy my ice cream! My father arrived after travelling all the way from Kent and walking up from Pinner station. He was always pleased to see me and would throw his arms around me. All I could say was 'Daddy, Daddy, can I have two pence?' and I went to put it back on the office table. The nurse caught me putting it back and said I could not go to communion until I had been to confession. I was badly upset because I had every intention of putting the money back. I felt I had been treated unjustly and I am sure this is the reason why it has always stuck in my mind. My father understood and will still tease me about it to this day.

Like the rest of the children I wanted attention. I had my 'moments', as my mother called them. I had to wear glasses, which I hated. One day I decided to hide them in the blanket cupboard. I had everyone looking for them. After about a fortnight I gave up and retrieved them from the blankets.

One Saturday, a visitor brought a dog to the ward to visit one of the children, and I was petrified of this dog. So I went and hid in the sluice. I wanted to stay there until the dog had gone. The nurse told me not to be so silly and to go back and play in the playroom. For a long time I used to dream about this dog. It's only in later life that I've got over my fear of dogs. In fact I'm quite fond of them now.

The drive leading to my ward was made of tarmac, and I often used to fall over when I walked up and down. Sometimes I would graze my knees or bruise myself. One day I didn't like the colour of my hand with a bruise across it. So I decided to try and scrub it clean with a nail brush and carbolic soap. It took me a few weeks to understand why it wouldn't come clean. Until then I was scrubbing it and getting very cross and frustrated!

St Vincent's Hospital had a small school where the teacher did her best to educate us in very limited conditions. Sister Kelly, the headmistress, always had faith in me and believed that I was intelligent. We had exams every term and she could not understand why I always came bottom of the class. Eventually she discovered that the effort of going to physiotherapy and keeping up with my schooling was too much for me. So Sister Jo, the ward sister, kept me in bed for a fortnight before the exams so that I could get better marks. It worked!

Looking back I realise how much effort I had to make to prove that I was reasonably intelligent in spite of my disabled body.

We had to go to bed at about 5 p.m. because this was easier for the nurses. I would try and get out of it by telling Sister Jo that I was 'bothered' and asking her if I could help her – really so that I wouldn't have to go to bed. I would pull at her habit as I was crawling along. Sometimes I got away with it. At other times I was told to be a good girl and go to bed.

When I was at Pinner I was allowed to go to Mass at 7.30 a.m. if someone could push me in the wheelchair. I listened to the sisters saying morning prayer in Latin but could not understand a word of it. I had no idea at the time that this office would become an important part of my prayer life. I did like to hear the sisters singing.

At Pinner we did not go out much beyond the gates, although once a year we went to a party and a pantomime. We had very little contact with the outside world. My father wanted to have me home for a holiday and had to ask the matron if this would be possible. For some time the answer was no, because it would mean that the hospital would not get money for me for the two weeks I was away. I did not understand much about this at the time, but Father's face looked sad when he told me. I would have to wait a bit longer before I could visit. During the time I was at Pinner I went home twice.

On one of the occasions I was allowed home my father took my two youngest sisters and me to see the pantomime of *Peter Pan* as a special treat. We had to catch two buses and my father had to carry me. When we arrived I started to cry, 'I want to go home to my mother,' and was so distresssed he had to take us all back home. My sisters never saw *Peter Pan* and my father still teases me about it.

School

By the time I was nine, Sister Jo and my parents were thinking of somewhere else for me to go. St Vincent's was not really helping me with my speech and the standard of education was somewhat poor, though my teacher did try. I could read a little, which compensated for not being able to write. The sum total of my writing efforts was ten to fifteen words a morning, all of which went into the bin! I just could not control my dribbling and the paper got soaked. I was eight before I could write my first letter, and that was, 'Dear Mummy and Daddy, I hope you are well, love Liz'.

In 1956, I went to Stroud in Gloucestershire to continue my education as well as on-going treatment. St Rose's was at that time the only Catholic school offering specialist help to the physically disabled. There I was introduced to the typewriter which changed my life. Up to that moment, in all honesty, few people could read my writing.

When I first went to the school it was like a big house, but very soon we moved across the road to a much bigger new building. The opening was in May and I was in the band. We had a concert and when I was playing the triangle I wobbled and dropped it! Father has always teased me about this particular effort. It doesn't say a lot for someone who comes from a musical family!

At first when I went to St Rose's there was a physiotherapist there who was not experienced in the treatment of people with cerebral palsy. She gave me a pair of walking sticks to try and keep my arms down. She was also aware that I had speech problems and did try to give me some exercises for my tongue. Not long after this, a new physio and speech therapist came to the school.

At the age of twelve I was writing out my twelve times table. My form teacher remarked, 'You don't expect me to praise you for that, do you?' I was angry. I had put so much effort into it and at the time it appeared to me as if the exercise was of no value at all. Who would spend forty minutes writing out the twelve times table? I was wrong. My teacher looked at the typewriter and asked, 'How about this?' Thus began my proper education. At first it would take me about two hours to type half a page but I did get faster. Since then the typewriter has been my main means of putting my work down on paper, and people have found it easier to read what I was trying to say.

In those days there were no such things as guards to go over the keyboard so that you could lay your finger on the key you wanted without hitting other keys. You had to do it all the hard way, but learning to use the typewriter was the beginning of my proper education. I have a lot to thank my teacher for. Today, of course, children who cannot write are given a computer or some kind of communicator with which to express themselves when they are four or five years old – not twelve! Part of the result of my late start is that I am poor at spelling. I am sure it would have made the world of difference if I had started younger. The typewriter has given me more freedom. In time I could put my thoughts on paper, but – more important – people could understand what I was writing about. Looking back, I had no idea then that I would be writing my life story on a computer with a guard across the keys. I wish I had had this facility long ago to enable me to express myself and thus communicate more easily.

I realise now that I was very behind for a girl of my age. I can remember a geography lesson. We had to fill in a stencilled map. If I told the teacher where to put information she would do it for me. This was because I was unable to put the mark where I wanted it to go due to my lack of hand control. I put Africa into South America. After the test she said, 'Liz, tell me, where is Africa?' I had to admit that at the age of fourteen, I didn't have a clue. I just about knew where Great Britain was.

However, the headmistress had some very funny ideas. There was an occasion when my mother wanted to come to see me when it was not a visiting day. I was given permission, but I was told not to tell the other children. I was so excited that I told my friends. I was overheard by a member of staff who went back and reported me to the headmistress. The headmistress was furious and told me my mother could not come. I wrote and told my mother that it must be God's will. (I had learnt at school that everything that was hard was God's will.) The headmistress used to read our letters before they were posted and would not allow me to send this letter. I had to write and tell the truth. I remember when the holidays came I thought Mother would be cross with me. Not at all. She just wanted to see her daughter, but didn't expect me to be treated differently from anyone else.

Because it was a Catholic school, the development of our faith was given serious consideration. We had morning and night prayers in the dormitory. We had prayers at assembly before school began and the rosary was often said at the end of the day. When we did not have Mass in school, I sometimes went to Mass at the convent in the morning. At that time I may not have understood the wording of the Mass because it was in Latin, and I certainly did not understand all the readings as I had not studied them. I just enjoyed going to Mass and receiving Holy Communion when it was possible. The headmistress only allowed me to do this if I went to bed at 7 p.m. the night before. One of the things I remember was that if I went to early Mass I had a cup of tea and a breath of air before breakfast.

At the age of twelve, I received the sacrament of confirmation. We went to the parish church and my father came to join me for the day. I cannot remember who my sponsor was, or even being prepared for confirmation. However, I do remember choosing the name Anne because it was the name of Our Lady's mother.

When I left school my standard of education was considered insufficient to take GCE or a Pitman's typing examination. I myself thought that my typing was up to standard. All my friends were doing typing exams and I was determined not to be left out. I knew how to tabulate and set out a letter and I could copy-type so I pleaded with the teacher to let me try. I was given half an hour extra. However, the teacher knew my standard was below par. I could only use two fingers so she was not at all surprised that I failed. For me this was an important test because it brought home to me the co-ordination problem I had with my hands. There was no way I could pass the exam; I could only type ten words a minute!

The reason I tell this story is that disabled people are often left behind in education because they have to put so much energy into learning activities which able-bodied people have no problems with at all. As I have grown older I have had to learn to bear this in mind and not get cross with myself when I do not know as much as I think I ought to know, and when the learning process itself is slow and laborious.

I enjoyed typing; it was an outlet for me. However, typing caused a problem for my physiotherapist. Because I was putting so much energy into typing I was not doing enough writing which is a different kind of movement. My teacher and the physiotherapist nearly came to blows! I was not the only person in this situation; most of us having physiotherapy shared the same problem. I compensated by going to the physiotherapy department after school and practising writing on a board to try to develop more hand control. I think this made everybody a little happier.

As I became older, physiotherapy and speech therapy were very important elements of life at school. Then a new physio-therapist, who was Bobath-trained, joined the staff of the school. 'Bobath-trained' refers to a type of physio that is more geared for people with neurological problems. The first thing she did was to take my walking sticks away. 'Thank goodness for that!' commented the headmistress. 'Liz would have taken somebody's eye out before long.' During physiotherapy I learned to make tea, to fasten buttons and tie shoe-laces. This was hard work for me but as long as I tried each morning, I did not get into trouble if I was late for breakfast.

Until I was twelve, going up and down stairs on my own was accomplished sitting on my bottom. This way was much easier. The physio would supervise my practice walking up and down steps, in the treatment room as well as the steps in the garden. By the time I left school I could do this, although I still needed to hold on to the rail in order to keep my balance.

During the summer holidays, my brother Vincent and I would go away to Princes Risborough for a holiday. We would stay at a school run by some nuns. There would be about ten of us, all disabled; we had a great time! We went on outings and played games in and out of the house. I still keep in contact with some of those people who were once my holiday companions. In fact one of them who had serious cerebral palsy managed to go to university and was able to lecture for a while. She's now married to an Anglican vicar and seems very happy.

Another remembered happening of the school holidays was that at home I shared a room with my sisters, Clare and Ursula. They liked me to tell them stories about school. I remember telling them about the sisters and the physiotherapist. During one holiday I wasn't doing my exercises and Clare decided to write a letter to the school so that I would get 'told off' when I went back. I can't remember whether I did get 'told off' or not, but the physio did not forget Clare's letters!

Clare was able to use a sewing machine when she was about fourteen to make her own clothes. I recall feeling very cross and upset because she could use the machine and I could not. I hid in the bathroom and cried. I think this was the first time my mother had to deal with my reaction of anger and frustration at my own inability. Mother tried to placate me by explaining that I would hurt myself if I tried to use the machine. My teenage years presented many other similar disappointments to be faced.

If I was naughty or misbehaved, like most children I was punished. One day I was being greedy, wanting too much tea to drink and I think I got into a tantrum. Father carried me upstairs, put me on the bed and smacked me. On another occasion in the holidays, my brothers and sisters were sliding down the banisters and I was kneeling at the bottom, egging them on in my own way. My mother walked in through the front door and gave them all a slap on the leg. I sat there watching, thinking she wouldn't hit me. She came to me and said, 'And you, you are the oldest. You ought not to be encouraging them.' She gave me a slap on the leg too. So, when my parents could, they treated me in the same way as the others.

During one holiday my mother was in hospital. I think she was expecting Mary, and in my own little way I wanted to keep the house tidy. I was crawling about trying to tidy the bedroom and sweep the floor. I have not yet forgotten the physical effort this entailed. But I enjoyed it; I was helping, however small the result.

When it was time for lunch or tea it was my job to go and tell my father. I would say 'Father, it is dinner time' and he would say 'What is?' and he would gently sit me down in a chair, and then go and tell Mother I would not come for dinner. To this day I have never worked out what answer I was supposed to give him. I think he was just pulling my leg.

It was the last day of the school holidays. Mother had promised me I could go to the shop on my own before I went back to school. I think, out of love, she was anxious about my going and thus the outing was put off until the last day. I was overjoyed when she said I could go to the butcher for some liver for Father's tea. He had gone to school and I would not see him again until half-term. I was very careful to cross the road and went into the shop and managed to buy the liver. Mother was pleased that I had managed it, but more relieved that I had come home safely. I was thrilled that I could go back to school and tell them that I had been to the shop on my own. I was eleven years old.

I kept contact with the physio. She left the school two years ago. I am going to talk about my speech problems in another chapter but while I was at school my speech therapist helped me considerably. Sadly she died two years after I left. She was a very special person. She did not believe in God. I can still remember her saying to me, 'We came from the apes and, therefore, there's no life after death.' She was one of the kindest and most sincere people I have ever met. I always had a great admiration for her for working in a Catholic environment and respecting everything that happened in the school. The headmistress did not agree with my getting on with the speech therapist so well and tried to tell me that she was a bad influence on me. I am afraid I did not believe the headmistress and took no notice of what she said.

Work Experience

When I completed school as a pupil I was given the opportunity to return to get some work experience. I went back for a year, working with the children in the kitchen and in the laundry. My ambition was to continue to work in the laundry because one of the things I could do well was ironing and I quite enjoyed it! What the headmistress wanted me to learn was that I did not have the strength to work in the laundry.

I loved working with the children, helping them to get up in the morning and, in so far as I could, at meals. I pushed them in wheelchairs to their classrooms and encouraged them to do their own pushing. Some of the children who had cerebral palsy asked me how old I was when I began to walk and talk. They were looking for encouragement and I had to be very careful because no two people with cerebral palsy are alike. When I was unsure I would check with the physiotherapist and speech therapist to make sure that what I did say was correct.

I had my own room and could go and come as I pleased when I was not on duty. I used to go to the library and sometimes I would take myself shopping. Because people couldn't understand what I was saying I had to get somebody to write down what I wanted before I went. One thing I did at the age of sixteen was to have my first cup of coffee on my own in a cafe in the town.

I got on quite well with the staff but I did find it hard to keep up with all that we had to do. Sometimes we would go out together and two of us joined the Legion of Mary. That was good for me because we had to visit people in the town and thus my circle of acquaintances grew. On occasion it was embarrbassing because the people I had gone to visit felt more sorry for me when the intention was I should support them. I had to try and take it in my stride. Sometimes I had to bite my lip!

While I was working at the school I was paid a weekly wage. The year went very quickly and everybody had to begin to think what would happen when the time came for me to leave. Everybody was telling me that I was too disabled to do a proper job.

Reflection

Over the years I have come across a number of disabled children who spent their early life in a hospital. As in my own case there were probably a number of reasons for this. There was no Catholic school or hospital near where I lived, where I could get the treatment I needed. My parents had the other children as well as Vincent to think about, so they had to consider what was best all round.

When I was a child I did not really question why I was disabled. I knew no different as nearly all my peers were disabled in one way or another. However, the situation did hit me hard in my teens. Why could even my disabled peers do things I could not, such as write, speak normally and eat with their lips together? I would become upset and the headmistress would tell me that 'it was God's will for me'. At that time I just accepted it. I do believe suffering can be used in a positive way but one has to grow to a stage of maturity to understand such a premise.

Day schools for disabled children were very few and far between. If one came from a large family, other members of the family had to be looked after too and disabled children may take up more time than their siblings. In those days families did not have as much financial help as they do today. This meant that in many cases both parents may have had to go out to work, making it difficult to keep the disabled child at home.

Although I was happy at Pinner, we were kept away from the real world. As stated, we did not go beyond the hospital gates apart from outings round about Christmas time. This happened in most large institutions. In those days, children who were in such places were not encouraged to know what went on in the world outside the one in which they were living. That was in the early fifties. Today, in the nineties, disabled children are encouraged to be more aware of everyday life and have more opportunities to participate in that life.

I left school eventually at the age of seventeen but I would like to say a word about that. In some cases disabled children are able to go to an ordinary school and with a little help learn alongside their able-bodied peers. Where at all possible I think this should be encouraged. There are, of course, cases where realistically this is impossible; for instance, if a child needs special medical treatment or is really very seriously disabled. I personally think that these are probably the only reasons for going to a special school offering intensive treatment and care. However, even in a special school it is very important that the standard of education be high and there be opportunities for the children to be in contact with the outside world.

Unfortunately some special schools do not offer a high standard of education, and this again is a drawback. So if one has to go to a special school it is important to get the right balance between education and treatment. Looking back, although I would have liked to have gone to a school for children who were not disabled, I know that as things were in those days I did benefit from attending a school for physically disabled children.

2

Returning Home

When I finally left school, nobody was quite sure what would happen to me due to my severe disability. I was sent on an assessment course run by the Spastics Society which was meant to help determine my future.

Assessment

The assessment course was designed to see if I was capable of taking and doing a job, or at least to see what the possibilities were. I was asked to do activities which were physically beyond me at that time. I remember that when I came back I made a list of everything we had been asked to do so that I could send it to the physio in order that she could get people to practise before she launched them into the course another time. On the course, we were given all kinds of manual tasks to carry out, which I had never tried before; for example, trying to use a screwdriver and trying to put an electric plug together. I had never seen a plug undone before, let alone put it together. There were also some written tests in which I know I didn't do very well.

I am pleased to say that the kind of assessment we had back in the early sixties has been changed. The Spastics

Society now has a different approach to the assessment and the whole family is now involved. This type of assessment gives a clearer picture of the person's situation at that time of their life.

The outcome of my assessment was that it was felt I was too disabled to be trained for a job. Looking back I believe that this was probably true but at the time it was very hard to accept. Why could I not work like other members of my peer group? I had to accept the fact that I was going back to live at home with my family, and to a work centre for people with cerebral palsy.

At Home

Once I had returned home from the assessment, I was told about a retreat for disabled school-leavers taking place at the end of August, at St Elizabeth's, Much Hadham, in Hertfordshire. We were a nice bunch of kids; helpers were invited to come and look after us and make the retreat with us.

We had three conferences a day and a reading-room where we could go and read quietly on our own. However, if someone was blind or could not hold a book a helper would read to them. As happened at most forms of retreat in those days, we were encouraged to keep as silent as we could. We only talked to each other after lunch, when we normally went for a walk in the beautiful grounds that surrounded St Elizabeth's.

What was important about the retreat was that the same input was given to us as would have been given to any other group of youngsters. I can still remember that it gave me a better understanding of how the Gospels could influence my life. Thinking about it now, it seems odd that after all the Masses I had attended and all the times I had heard the

21

Gospels read and preached, it was only now that they were beginning to speak to me. However, after this retreat, I knew I could try and live out the Gospels in my everyday life.

Once home, one of the things my mother wanted to do for me was try to get me some more education, but there seemed to be nowhere for me to go – not even within the Spastics Society. We learned later that the last year I had spent at school could have been paid for by the local authority and I could have had more schooling. I know I would have appreciated it.

The result of my assessment was that I should go to a work centre for people with cerebral palsy. I returned home from Devon where I had been assessed and had to wait until January before I could go to my new place of work. This was a difficult time trying to settle down at home and getting to know my family better. I had not lived at home, apart from the holidays, since I was four, and this is very different from living and growing up at home all the time. I loved my family dearly but they did not know me. Neither did I know them as well as they knew each other. To my brothers and sisters I was their disabled sister and therefore my parents made allowances but did try to make as little difference as possible between us all. My brothers and sisters soon learned that I could play up and want my own way just like them.

I wanted to become more independent and decided to try to go to evening classes but Mother would not hear of it; she was too worried lest I damage myself. She did let me go to some talks on history at the local Baptist church and encouraged me to join the library.

At that time, it was not the norm for disabled people to go to work or to a normal evening class. I missed my friends. I must have driven my parents mad. My mother had a job as a home-help organiser and I can remember she usually came home at lunch-time to prepare the dinner and make sure that I was all right. She never took her coat off.

When I went to live at home, like every school-leaver I had to have my money sorted out. In those days there were not the benefits for disabled people as there are today. I had to go each week on a Friday to collect my unemployment benefit. I could not get sickness benefit, as I was only seventeen. We were living in Purley by this time. My mother took me to East Croydon Labour Exchange to sign on and collect my unemployment benefit. To start with, the lady I saw was quite pleasant and understanding. We explained to her that I was waiting for a place at the work centre, but I don't think she really understood. When I started going on my own she began to get a bit unpleasant and would ask me 'if I had found a job'. I had to try and explain that I could not do a job. In the end I would get so upset that my mother went to fetch my money for me. I cannot remember how much it was but I would give Mother some for my keep at home. She didn't take much but she wanted to help me to manage my money.

In the evenings she would sometimes take me out for a walk round the block and nine times out of ten I would press my claim for greater independence such as joining a youth club. One of the jobs I did was to collect my sister, Felicity, from school. She did not really like holding my hand but I made her do so as we crossed the road. I bet her children react to her in the same way as she did to me because no sister or brother likes to be seen having to walk with their older sibling.

The Work Centre

In January 1964, I started at the work centre, where I either made coathangers or spent my time packing crayons into boxes. One of the jobs of the manager of the centre was to find factories which would offer us contract work suitable to our different physical abilities. I was bored, really bored! My mind was unused. There were four of us in the same boat and we did our best to amuse ourselves. While I was there I asked the manager if I could start a current affairs group because it seemed to me that we were somewhat behind in our knowledge of what was going on in the world. It went very well.

On occasion I brought some of my friends home. Sometimes we had transport provided, other times we travelled by bus – a lot depended on my state of health. As we did not have to be at the centre till ten, sometimes my brother Paul would drop me there as he went past on the way to his office. There was a catch in this. If I made his bed, he would give me a lift.

One of my great friends was Carol. She was very badly disabled and had real difficulty in speaking. She actually spoke better when she was lying on the floor, so we would go into the front room and chat for hours. Mother would bring us tea and I helped Carol. We had a good laugh. She could eat better than I could, but could not feed herself, so I used to feed her. It was a bit like the blind leading the blind. The food sometimes went everywhere except where it should. Carol became a Catholic and I was her sponsor. It was good to be with her when she was received into the Church. Being her sponsor I felt I was responsible for making her feel welcome and at ease in the Catholic Church. To this day we still keep in contact.

There was also a lady at the work centre who was about fifty. She had little or no education and could not read, so I tried to help her to read. She had had a very hard life and nothing had been done to help her. There was another severely disabled girl called Pat. She was about seventeen and I used to feed her at dinner times. I enjoyed that. I felt I was doing something useful.

I didn't have many activities outside my home life, but being a member of the work centre I was able to go to a club where we had table tennis, music, a coffee bar and many other activities. Now and again we would go on an outing. On a Friday night I went swimming. I enjoyed that very much. Sometimes on a Saturday I would get the bus and go ten-pin bowling with some of the people from the club. We had many a laugh because none of us could really bowl the ball.

As the manager always said, my heart was not really in the work centre. It most certainly was not! I was bored stiff there. I was not using my brain. I wanted to get away and get some more education and that's how I ended up in Bristol.

However, that was not the end of work centres for me. I still had to return to a work centre in Bristol part-time. That was even more boring. I had to tear postage stamps and if I was lucky I was able to have a go at making coathangers. It seemed harder to get contract work there.

Reflection

It is important to remember that I had been lucky enough to have had a Catholic education. What about all the other children who had not been so fortunate? It is natural for teenagers to fight against their faith but I feel my doubts and struggles came later on in life. Some of the people on the school-leavers' retreat and youngsters at the work centre had never had an opportunity for their faith to be nourished or for it to become part of their lives. However, in my case I know that most of the people who helped me understood my faith and surrounded me with love and maybe the way they lived out their faith made an impression on me. Some of the young people did have a chance to go to Lourdes; this was probably the only occasion when they could be with people with whom they could share the same experience of faith. I feel sure that some of them had received no religious education or even attended their local parish Sunday school, as it was called in those days. Although I am a Catholic, I believe one must respect the faith of people of other denominations. Some of the people at the centre came from different religious backgrounds.

I can recall when I was at the work centre being teased about having faith. Looking back now, I can see that the others had not had similar opportunities as myself with regard to faith. Life is hard enough for any teenager, but maybe a life without faith to provide secure roots and foundations is that bit more difficult. However, if you are trying to live in a society which is not geared for people who are disabled it must be so much harder for those who have no faith to fall back on. I must stress here that the people to whom I refer are not those whose circumstances cause them to lose their faith, but children and youngsters who have not had a chance to know what having faith is all about.

One of the disadvantages of growing up away from home and then suddenly trying to become part of the family in one's teens is that a disabled person will have developed their own way of life in accordance with their disability, but parents and family will be unaware of how much or how little the disabled person is able to do or not do. This can be a great strain on both sides. When able-bodied teenagers go out in the evening, for example, a good parent will let them go but, of course, worry till their son or daughter returns. When a disabled teenager goes out alone or with friends, parents are much more anxious because they are not used to seeing them so independent. Time and patience are needed from both parents and children alike. In my own case, it was not easy as I was determined to be as independent as possible but, I have to admit, I often wanted to run before I could walk! I must have driven my parents 'round-the-bend' at times. Now we can look back and laugh. Obviously they wanted the best for me but perhaps their anxiety was all the more because they had a disabled son as well.

3

Bristol

I went to the Spastics Society headquarters for assessment to see where would be the best place for me to go. I saw a doctor and an educational psychologist. In the course of conversation the psychologist said, 'If you got drunk you might walk straight – try it one day but don't tell anyone I told you to try it.' I have never put this to the test! It was decided that I should go to Bristol to live in a Spastics Society hostel.

The Hostel

At the hostel there were about eight residents and the warden, who was married. While I was there I had a bit of a problem which had a great impact on my outlook on life. The warden's husband worked at the docks and had his own boat at the harbour. I got on well with both of them but neither was the kind of person with whom I would choose to spend time, as we had nothing in common. He would often chat with me as we passed on the stairs. To start with I thought nothing of it, but then he started to make passes at me and tell me how attractive and clever I was and that he could talk to me unlike some of the others in the hostel. One day he opened his trousers and exposed himself. I felt uncomfortable and

28

uneasy. I was very naive and although I should have known, I did not really understand what it was about. No one had really told me about the facts of life. One day when I was at the work centre, I became very upset and confused over this and told one of the staff. I had no idea that this one event was going to cause me so much misery and unhappiness as well as being a growing-point in my life.

The manager at the centre called head office in London. My social worker and one of the staff who employed the wardens for the Spastics Society came down. I told them my story. Until this day I can still hear the social worker saying 'We do believe you.' I replied, 'I don't mind if you don't. The truth will tell in the end.' As soon as we were alone she ticked me off and said I should have contacted her direct. I had only met her twice before so did not feel I knew her that well. She was more concerned about that than what had taken place.

I was due to go into hospital back in Surrey. At least this meant I could get away from it all. I worried about the incident a lot because I had not told my parents what had been going on. If I had told them I would never have gone back to Bristol. The social worker came to see me in hospital. I had very mixed feelings about her coming to see me because I knew she would find something to chastise me about.

She did come one day to tell me that the couple running the hostel had split up. I said to her, 'I'm very sorry but I always told you the truth would tell in the end.' Inside I felt a great sense of relief. When I was better I returned to the hostel and eventually a new warden couple were appointed and I got on very well and managed to carry on doing my studies at Bristol Polytechnic.

That was not the end of my saga of Bristol and the social worker. One day I had a sore throat and I decided to pop along to the doctor. He signed me off work and told me to go home and rest. I went back to the hostel and I told the lady who was in charge for the day and then went off to bed. When the warden came back that evening she was furious and told me I had to go to the work centre the next day. I went to the work centre and I happened to tell one of the staff that I had been to the doctor and he had given me a certificate to be off work. When the person realised this he took me back to the hostel and explained that I had a certificate and I should not be at work.

Again the warden was furious and she telephoned my social worker to tell her that I was playing up. The social worker phoned me and told me I had to go home to my parents the next day, until she could sort out what to do with me. At that time the warden herself was suffering from the menopause and every now and then she got things out of perspective.

When I arrived at Purley I rang the social worker from the station and asked her what was going to happen. I also told her that my mother was not well. I can recall her saying, 'Well, you can go home and look after her then.' I mentioned to her that I was missing college. Her comment was, 'You can contact the college and find out what you are meant to be doing and study at home.'

When I arrived home my parents were understanding and thought it was a storm in a teacup. The social worker came to see my parents about a fortnight later. After a discussion and lecture about me behaving myself, she said that the warden would have me back. She also said that she wouldn't be working with me any more and that I would have to go and see a psychiatric social worker.

I returned to Bristol on the following Sunday. My mother came with me. We had a cup of tea and a chat with the warden who apologised and said she had been a bit overwrought and suggested that we put the incident behind us and begin again. I remember feeling very nervous and alone for a few days but it did not take me long to get back to normal. As far as I was concerned it really was a storm in a teacup.

When I was younger I was not very good at dealing with conflict and so could not cope with being unable to get on with my social worker. People had tried to tell me gently but I did not want to believe it. When she finally left Bristol she told me she could not keep in contact with someone whom she had made go through so much.

It was only then that I realised that in some cases it is impossible for two people to get on with each other. It took me a while to get over this. I was offended, but at the same time it was a growing-point that I do not think I shall ever forget.

Graham

I had another interesting experience in Bristol and that was my first experience of someone falling in love with me. Graham lived in Bath and sometimes came to Bristol to see some of his friends. Apparently we met at a function we were both at, but I cannot recall this. After meeting me the first time, he asked me if I would like to go out with him. I accepted his invitation and we went for a car ride around the Cotswolds. He told me he had a job and he was living with his mother, and that he was forty years old. I was only twenty-two. I felt he was old enough to be my father!

I ought to say that Graham also suffered from cerebral palsy, and he could barely walk. He had very good manual dexterity and his speech was normal, although his head was never still. Because Graham could not walk, we could not really go out except by car and I cannot recall the number of times we went to Coombe Downs in Bath. We used to sit in the car and talk about everything, but I only liked Graham as a friend.

I was rather taken by surprise when he began making love to me. In fact I felt very uneasy because I knew I did not feel the same way as he did. He used to tell me to take it easy and not to be afraid, it would come. I felt very torn about this, because I did not want to hurt him but I also did not want to pretend that I loved him when I knew I did not. I tried to explain to him but it was a bit like hitting my head against a brick wall. At that time I did not have anyone I could talk to about it, so I soldiered on.

However, Graham was getting impatient and he knew my social worker was coming to see me. He hung around the hostel in the hope that he would be able to have a talk with her. He thought she would be able to get me to change my mind. He did not know, at that time, that my social worker was the last person in whom I had confidence. She did try to talk to me but I cannot recall the conversation. I was very angry with Graham for going to see her because this was not her business. Graham did not know, at that time, that my social worker 'had it in for me'.

It was no good. Graham still kept trying to persuade me to have a relationship with him. For my part it was agony, I knew he was frustrated, he wanted to settle down. I tried to explain to him that we were too disabled to manage life together, quite apart from the fact that I did not want it. (In those days society would have considered it to be inappropriate for disabled people to be married.) There was another problem about which I had not told Graham. I had had a hysterectomy. That was why I had been in hospital eighteen months before. His face dropped and I could see I had really hurt him, but I tried to tell him that there had really been no need for him to know because on my side the relationship was not developing. He was devastated and I felt full of guilt for the next few months. I had hurt someone but I was also being honest.

Graham did not see me for about two weeks but then he began to come to the hostel again. Fortunately for me, I was leaving Bristol in about a month's time and I broke the news to Graham on one of these occasions. He knew the day I was going and he came to say goodbye. I remember my emotions were very mixed but I have not seen him since then. However, I have heard that he found an able-bodied lady and is now married. The relief I feel I would never be able to explain.

A few weeks ago we had a family get-together and we were discussing our boyfriends. I did not think my parents knew about my relationship with Graham. My sisters told me they did know and had nearly had a heart attack when they realised that I was going out with someone as disabled as Graham. I don't think they had any idea what I was going through as I tried to get him out of my life. I think I must have mentioned it to my sisters as I cannot recall telling my parents what was happening in Bristol with Graham.

Bristol Life

At the Bristol Polytechnic I studied the British constitution at 'A' Level, economics and public affairs, and commerce. This may appear a strange choice of subjects but the reason I selected them was I knew very little about any of them and I wanted to be better informed. It was good to have the chance of studying again because I knew I had missed out on a lot at school and I was keen to broaden my mind.

I got on quite well with the other residents living in the hostel but tension was created because I was going to college. They thought I was 'toffee-nosed'. They were lovely people but because of their upbringing and disabilities they were not intellectual.

In Bristol there was a very good St Vincent de Paul society and one of the members was a teacher. When he discovered what I was doing he offered to help me with my essays. He would either come to the hostel or I would go to his house. These were good days because we would get through a lot of work as I would plan the essay beforehand and then we would have supper. When I was at home my brother, Martin, let me dictate my work to him if I had a deadline. We would wait till everyone had gone to bed and work with records playing in the background and unlimited cups of coffee. Those were good days. I really enjoyed working in this way with Martin; he is a good sport. When it came to taking my exams I dictated them to the physiotherapist who worked at the work centre because she thought it wouldn't be a good idea for me to type for five hours. It was hard work dictating but I was overjoyed when I passed the exams.

Also while I was in Bristol I started to write a book of prayers about everyday situations in the world of the disabled. For all sorts of reasons I kept pushing it to the back of my mind. In 1975 I turned to it once more and tried to find a publisher. In 1980 a well-known publisher showed an interest but felt that it did not have a potentially wide readership. A great friend of mine kindly paid for the Carmelites in Quidenham to print it. I am told people have found it helpful. This pleased me. Not that I wrote it for my own glory, but I wrote it to encourage others. One of the prayers I wrote was about the work centre:

Monotonous Work

O Lord, I have to face the fact that my disability is too great for me to go to work in a factory, office or shop like my friends. I have to go to a work centre and do the most monotonous jobs like putting crayons in boxes, tearing stamps or any other kind of job that the management committee may be able to find. I hate it all, Lord. I am so bored and frustrated. What future is there in a centre for me? Sometimes I feel I am just here to be occupied and to be out of the way. I am not using my mind and that part of me is not disabled, Lord. Lord, if I have to depend on a work centre for work all my life, please teach me not to go round the bend. If there is no alternative for me, and it is your will that I am at a work centre, please turn my frustration into something constructive and fruitful so that when people meet me they will not see the suffering and frustration that you have sent me, that I want to accept. But let them see me at peace so that by being in contact with me they may get a glimpse of the unchanging love that you have for each and every one of us. Lord, I am weak and human, and cannot do anything without you. So please come and take over, especially when I am at work. I depend entirely on you, Lord.

When I was in Bristol I can remember helping out at a school for children with learning difficulties. I would go down there on Saturday mornings and encourage the children in whatever way I could. I loved it but did not agree with all the principles and methods used to educate the children, but I was not in a position to make any comment. The regime was far too strict; some tender loving care would not have gone amiss. Sometimes I left the school with very mixed feelings.

A priest friend of mine, Father Austin Garvey, who started the retreats for disabled people at Much Hadham, told me of the Fraternity for Handicapped People based in France. While I was in Bristol I became involved in the local parish. I told them of this fraternity and so we invited my friend down to talk to us about it. Shortly after this we managed to get our own group under way.

We had problems with transport and members of the St Vincent de Paul society helped us to go to the parish centre. We were from all denominations and all had different disabilities. I had great fun with Father Francis trying to get him to understand what I wanted from him in order to encourage the other members to take on more responsibility instead of letting the able-bodied members do it all.

The aim of the fraternity is to encourage disabled people to take responsibility for one another and seek ways of living out the gospel. The older ones were to look after the younger ones and the more severely disabled. The day I left Bristol the physically disabled were giving a party for the mentally handicapped. (We no longer use this term but speak of them as people with learning difficulties or disabilities.) I remember feeling very moved; I felt I had achieved something in the church. The group continued on for a few years after I had left.

Reflection

I was at Bristol for three and a half years and I really changed as a person. First of all I had that bad experience with the husband of the warden. I had had very few relationships with males in my childhood apart from the family, and for about a year I was nervous towards men, but I soon overcame it.

I would like to mention here that in those days it was well known that Catholic schools did not always tell pupils the facts of life. Parents often gave their children the Catholic Truth Society pamphlet called *My Dear Daughter* which was meant to tell you all you needed to know but there was little discussion between parents and children. Apart from being a late developer I am sure this was an added contribution to my unfortunate experience.

I learned that in this life there were some people you would not get on with; personalities can clash and there is nothing you can do about it. Getting through the hurt to understanding, and realising that in some cases this happens, takes time to come to terms with – but it is not the end of the world.

When I went to college I was meeting and working alongside able-bodied people for the first time in my life. I cannot recall any major misunderstanding because I happened to be disabled. Also because it was the first time I had organised something for other people (for example, the transport), I had to learn to give and take and make sure I did not leave anybody out. It was the first time I had responsibility for other people. Understandably, people who helped me with the group did not always agree with my ideas. I had to learn that it was all right – people do not always agree with each other. This was something else that helped me to grow up and learn to work with other people.

The biggest lesson of all was that no matter what I thought about myself, one person considered I was worthy of his falling in love with me. I could not reciprocate so I had to live with the fact that I had quite rightly turned him down but at the same time had to acknowledge it is perfectly natural for people to fall in love. I had been involved in something that occurred in everyday life and I learned a great deal from it.

A big plus from my going to Bristol was my becoming involved in the outside world and developing my own personality. Very often disabled people are overprotected and are not encouraged to develop their own potential. Nowadays, disabled people are given more opportunities at an earlier age and I think this should be encouraged as much as possible.

4

Life in Hostels

Moving on

I have lived in several different parts of the country: Huddersfield, Pinner, Stroud, Purley, Bristol. When I was twenty-four I moved to Croydon because I wanted to get a flat of my own. Croydon's housing department, without having seen me, decided I was too disabled to live on my own, so I moved into a residential home in South Croydon where I could live as independently as possible. Help was there if I needed it but I made my own decisions. Most of the residents were very ill or dying; understandably they did not have much life in them! I do remember the odd interesting conversation; for example, one with a man who was suffering from multiple sclerosis and who had two children.

When I was living at the home I realised I could not hold down a full-time job. Due to my disability I do not have sufficient energy to enable me to function long enough for a full-time job or even a part-time one; I would be rather unreliable. I realised this in my twenties and so I took the alternative route to devote as much time as I could to voluntary work. I used to travel up to Bayswater to help out in a shop. It was partly an antique shop and partly a charity shop for the Saturday Venture Club. I caught the train from

East Croydon station and then travelled by the underground to Bayswater. It was the first time I had such a responsibility. When I was working on my own in the shop, I worried in case anybody picked up an antique when I was dealing with another customer. Another concern was checking the money at the end of the day. If it was my job to lock the shop I would go back three or four times to make sure it was secure. I think this was partly because I wasn't used to such a responsibility. I had a good time there dealing with the public and meeting all kinds of people. We were visited by many tourists, especially Americans, and they were very interesting to deal with. We would also meet other people who just came to get some bargains so they could take them away to sell in their own antique shops and make a profit.

I embarked on another venture at that time. Jackie, a friend of mine, ran the Saturday Venture Club for physically disabled and able-bodied children. At that time most of the children were thalidomide victims. Before I came along the club folded up and Jackie asked me if I would help get it going again. Our meeting place was the Tiny Tim Centre in Victoria.

It was my job to make contact with the parents, find the voluntary helpers and organise the transport. We did normal club activities and went on outings. The club ran from 10 a.m. to 4 p.m. and there was a canteen but the children brought their own packed lunch. The Inner London Education Authority (ILEA) gave us a grant, and we were responsible to the youth officer who gave no end of support and with whom I got on like a house on fire.

After a short while we moved to the Sarah Siddons Youth Centre in Paddington. However, in the interim period I was asked to start a club at Worcester Park in Surrey. I had mixed feelings about this. I did wonder if I could manage; but another part of me saw it as a challenge, and at that time of my life if I was confronted with one I just went ahead and tried to see it through. This club took on the same format but the parents were more involved. I can remember the job I had contacting the Voluntary Workers Bureau for drivers and the local schools to ask if the sixth-form pupils could come and help. On the whole it worked out very well. We had to do our own fund-raising and therefore we ran jumble sales and at Christmas time organised carol singing. After about a year the club became more independent so it became autonomous. I became less involved and just sat on the committee. I think the club ran for another five years but in time I became so busy with other things that I lost contact.

Living in a Hostel

After about eighteen months I got tired of being in the home and wanted to move out to gain more independence. I heard about a hostel and Jackie agreed to pay my rent for a month until I proved that I could cope.

In the next eight years I lived in two hostels. One was in Baker Street with the Sisters of Charity; the other was in Kensington in an Anglican community. One of the things that struck me was that I had not realised before how big London is. I discovered that I could get where I wanted to go most easily on the underground. But I found the escalators very daunting, and had to depend on people to help me up and down them. This is what led me to write this prayer:

Standing at the Top of the Escalator

Dear Lord, I stood at the top of the escalator today and waited for one of your people to give me a hand down. So many times I said, 'Sir', 'Please, sir', 'Madam'. Of course, like the Good Samaritan, somebody came eventually to help me. Lord, if people have never met a spastic before, they often think spastics are drunk, because of the way they walk. Lord, teach us to be patient, to be understanding towards ignorant people. Help us, Lord, in these moments to remember the ones who cannot walk and be grateful that we can get around, even if it is a struggle.

From the two London hostels I was able to get to Mass most days. Both places had their tensions and drawbacks. I had been in the first hostel for eighteen months when a new sister-in-charge arrived. We did not see eye to eye. She wanted to use my disability as a way of helping the other girls do their good acts of charity, regardless of my feelings.

I was perfectly capable of making my own bed, and in those days I did my own washing and ironing. However, in the eyes of the sister-in-charge it was good for the other girls to exercise their charity on me. As a result I became very unhappy; it didn't make sense. All sorts of things were done for me which I did not need but I was not given help to put my suitcase in the lift which was something I should not even have attempted.

The last straw came when I went to a meeting about the Saturday Venture Club for disabled children, and on the way home three taxi-drivers would not pick me up, believing me to be drunk – my erratic walking again! When I arrived at the hostel the doors were locked and I had to call up the sister-in-charge. She treated me very coldly and didn't really listen to my explanation of what had happened. The next morning the mother superior summoned me and asked me why I had been late the night before. I repeated my story, but she didn't want to know and told me if it happened again I would have to go. I felt I had been treated unjustly. I just wanted to leave.

I began looking for somewhere else to live. I wanted to make sure that a similar occurrence didn't happen to another disabled person. So after I had left, Father Michael Garvey went to the mother superior to explain that the reason I had left was not to get revenge but to be my own mistress and to leave the doors open for others.

Bickersted House

In 1973 I moved into an Anglican hostel called Bickersted House. It was a very small hostel, with somewhere between twelve and eighteen residents plus the warden's family: Mary and John and their two children. We were encouraged to live as a community, sharing the household chores.

I had two things to struggle with. I was the only disabled person living there though there was someone who had a mild form of cerebral palsy. The other thing was being a Catholic; the others were Anglican. I had heard some good reports about this hostel, so I decided to try it. I was so devastated by what I had been through at the other hostel that anything was better than going on living there. Mondays were community nights. We had a Eucharist at 6.30 p.m., supper and then a community meeting.

I was expected to attend the Monday Eucharist. This was a source of conflict. As a Catholic I didn't feel it was right to receive Holy Communion in the Anglican rite and also this is what the Roman Catholic Church teaches. My feelings about this caused me a lot of uneasiness. I would go to 6 p.m. Mass at the Carmelites, and then rush back to be with the community for their Eucharist. I can remember using the time when they received communion for thanksgiving. If I was not able to get to Mass at the Carmelites, I can remember feeling very uneasy at the Anglican service, but, at the same time, I respected the way they lived out their faith. When we celebrated the Eucharist as part of the yearly birthday celebrations, as the years went by, I did receive the wine in their rite just out of respect as a member of their community.

Mary, who was the warden, and I were very honest with one another. It was agreed that I would pay extra rent so that the warden would cook me a midday meal. She told me what she expected of me and I also told her what my disability entailed. For instance, I could not be on the rota for cooking but I was well able to lay the table and help with the washing up once or twice a week.

On the whole the relationship between the residents and myself worked out well. They would give me a helping hand; for example, cutting up my food. I made many friends among the people who came to the community. But only a few kept in contact when they left. I enjoyed the freedom of having my own front-door key and being able to come and go as I wished.

When I was at Bickersted House I signed up with a very good GP, who took a great interest in my life. I really got to know her well and one day I went to her when I was feeling depressed. She agreed to give me something to help me as long as I came to see her for a short while on Fridays. People living in this hostel often seemed to suffer from depression, and my GP didn't believe I was that kind of person.

At the time I was feeling depressed about my brother, Vincent. The doctor helped me a great deal by letting me talk it through. We also covered some other worries I had, such as tiredness because I tended to do more than I could cope with.

However, she always encouraged me to use my mind. As my GP and responsible for my medical care, she always tried to give me the best and nothing seemed to be too much trouble for her. I owe her a great deal even though once or twice we didn't see eye to eye, but that was all right, we were both human. I was fortunate. Although I eventually moved out of her area she remained my GP until she retired.

While I was living at Bickersted I continued working at the charity shop in Bayswater. Very soon we had to move shop. We moved to a warehouse-type building in Westbourne Grove. It was a very big place. We had two display windows and were able to take a lot more goods than previously, including furniture. One of the good things about this shop was that we began to take on people who had had strokes or breakdowns; part of our work was to help their rehabilitation. This was an added bonus. We had great fun helping one another. Ron took a long time trying to say what he wanted to say and would much rather have written it down, but by the time I left he chatted away happily with the customers and would not let them get away with anything.

Jackie had overall responsibility and would come in two or three times a week to see that everything was in order, but I had quite a say in the running of the shop. It was up to me to tell everybody what to do. We also had people come in to help us sort out the clothes. They were a great asset and very good company. I hope I was fair to the workers as well as to the customers. When I began to be involved with the Have-A-Go Club, that was added to the charities we supported.

Before I knew it I was busy running another Saturday Venture Club in Paddington. The club took the same form as the one in Surrey, and ILEA gave us a great deal of support. Soon we obtained a grant to pay a full-time leader. He and I were meant to work together but it was not always easy. I think he felt that because he was able-bodied and a teacher he did not really need me around. We had one or two disagreements at the management committee but I must confess the committee did give me a great deal of support. I was not very happy with this new situation and began to consider giving up.

I had been in the hostel about three years when I started running the holiday project that we held at the same centre (see the next chapter). One day the warden at the centre failed to get me on the phone. She panicked and contacted the social services. A social worker came to see me and suggested that I have a home help. When the home-help organiser came, I asked her whether the home help would do my mending. She said, 'No!' I would still have to rely on my friends.

I think this is a good example of how people in authority do not understand practical situations. If you cannot sew a button on, what are you supposed to do? I was powerless and trapped. In 1978, an occupational therapist from the local borough came to see me. She arranged for me to have a telephone of my own with an amplifier.

For about seven years I was quite happy on the whole and then panic set in. I felt it was time for me to move on. I told the warden that I was looking for somewhere else to live. Sometime later Mary invited me to have lunch with her. I had the feeling that she was going to ask me to leave and I was right. She felt I was too disabled to go on living there. She felt I ought to be in a home with other disabled people. I was angry and hurt. How could she do this to me when she knew I was looking for some other place to live? The reason she felt I was more disabled was because I had lost my voice and had become incontinent. (I will write about this later.)

I went down to the church that evening and told a friend, who came back to my room and spent the evening with me.

Mary had given me two months' notice. I needed longer. This all happened in 1980. I contacted my social worker at Scope, who assured me that the warden had no right to put me out. I had done nothing wrong except that in the eyes of the warden I was becoming increasingly disabled. At that time Mary was expecting another baby.

In all sincerity I think Mary was fond of me. Here was a situation in which two human beings failed to handle a situation properly. We had been friends; we had been able to talk; I had supported Mary. This increased my anger and hurt. It took me months to get over it. I know Mary felt badly about it but she had to obey the instructions of her advisers. Later she came to see me in my flat. I always will remember the sense of relief I felt when I was able to say to her, 'Mary, you panicked!' Then we were able to discuss it. My anger started to go and after about two months we were back to being friends. Now although I see her only occasionally our good relationship continues.

Jane, the social worker, had been helping me for the past eighteen months in my effort to find some other accommodation. We looked at the Carr Gomm House which catered for people with problems but not my kind of problems. We also looked at what Scope had to offer, 'Good Neighbours' in Camberwell. I went there for a weekend but somehow I felt it was not for me. It was something of an institution.

Reflection

Looking back, I reflected on these experiences concerning living arrangements. Where was God in these situations? What was he trying to teach me? God was certainly in all the people involved. I think God showed me that in order to live in the outside world of so-called 'able-bodied' people, I would have to be willing to learn to make allowances. Many people simply do not know how to deal with disabled people or how to allow them to develop their own strengths and skills, yet at the same time be ready to help them when they really need help. Indeed many people are afraid of these situations. I often feel I cannot give much to others but maybe I am being asked to try to make myself more understanding towards others, by putting *them* at ease. I have to depend on the Holy Spirit for enlightenment and patience in order to try to carry this out.

5

My Calling

Awakening to My Calling

Trying to help other disabled people is what I seem to enjoy most, both in society and as a member of the Church. Every Christian has a calling; Roman Catholics usually call this an apostolate. Some people seem to spend most of their lives trying to work out what their apostolate is, instead of just getting on with the job at hand. Vocation is responding to an urge inside you. It is true that some people are clearer about what they should do than others; this 'urge' is stronger in some than others. God is in every Christian and in every aspect of life. Therefore a vocation is not necessarily centred upon 'church' in the restrictive sense. We are the Church and we can live and praise God just as much outside the church building as we can inside. A good example of what I am trying to say is Mother Teresa of Calcutta. She is a very holy person and spends a lot of time in prayer but her apostolate is among the poor and down-and-outs, seeing in them the beauty of God. She is an example to all of us as we go about our daily living knowing that God is always with us, whatever we are doing.

Because of my disability my apostolate varies according to my own physical needs as well as the needs of those around me. When I came to live in London I felt I wanted to do something to carry on helping people in the church. At that time, there was a priest in the diocese, Father David Wilson, who was responsible for people who were physically and mentally disabled. I was keen to do something specific for people with physical disabilities. He came to see me knowing that I wanted to work alongside the rest of the church for physically disabled people. He introduced me to Sister Kate who, like me, wanted to work for the physically disabled. One of the things I was doing at that time was to visit the residential homes in the diocese for people who were physically disabled. It was not all that successful so I was beginning to try to tackle the problem from the parish level.

I also tried to make contact with those disabled who were not getting any help to develop their faith. We therefore started a newsletter; one of its aims was to encourage priests to make contact with people in their parish who were disabled. We felt it might be a good idea to set up a group for the disabled in the Carmelite Church similar to the one I had started in Bristol. We advertised in the newsletter. Father Austin Garvey came to the meetings a few times to help us get going. We had about eight members.

One day we were offered the sacrament for the anointing of the sick. This was fine as a one-off event but then the group members decided that they would like the sacrament every month. At that time Canon Law only permitted it every two months. I had great difficulty in agreeing with the group. I was sure that this sacrament was a great source of grace but I felt it could be abused. There were not many people in the group who were sick. I was the most disabled person there and I wasn't sick. I felt it was wrong to have that sacrament every month. This was my personal opinion but being the leader of the group I had to support what the group felt. So I compromised by welcoming the sacrament every two months for the group but I abstained from receiving it that often myself. This was somewhat embarrassing but I felt it was important. The group loved having Mass together and the opportunity to share the gospel together. After the Eucharist we would have a cup of tea and a chat.

All this was very important but I could not persuade them to go and do something practical for other people who were disabled. One of the aims of the fraternity was to encourage the disabled to help themselves and other disabled people. The members of the group in Kensington were not interested in this kind of activity although they gained much from the meeting, so we just let it run as they wished. The group disbanded after nine years, after the coming of a new parish priest, and I was finding it hard to make the meeting each month as by that time I had left the parish. Looking back, I can see that I was not concerned that it folded because by that time the members of the group were well known in the parish and could join in other parish activities.

One of the things I did with Father David was to contribute to his newsletter for the disabled in Westminster diocese. In 1977, Father David arranged a weekend meeting for physically disabled people to look at their role in the church. This was held at Bedford. There were married couples as well as single persons there with their helpers. It was a weekend full of excitement, listening to how other people cope with their problems within the institutionalised church, and learning how different people dealt with them. We all agreed that we needed to educate our priests and the laity about the needs of disabled people.

A wide range of topics made up the agenda; for example, what it meant to be disabled, having a family, contraception, etc. We continued to meet for about two years and produced a document called, 'Disabled People to their Parish Priest'. We sent this out with the newsletter. Later there was a further version called 'All People Together'. This was distributed in the parishes by disabled people. There was a core group comprising Father David and three other disabled people including myself. The whole aim of the work was to integrate disabled people into parish life.

We had a day's retreat at Wembley shortly after publishing this text; there we met Mary and Tony. Tony was disabled and wanted to get involved. Father David asked him to become chairman. I felt a bit sore about this and told myself that this was done because he had normal speech but it wasn't this at all. Tony had a lot to give and remained chairman for quite a number of years. Soon after this Father David moved on and Father Chris Webb took his place. We continued to work, struggling to find our way forward and what we should be doing. Father Michael Garvey appeared on the scene with a special brief for the physically disabled and for the past few years I have been working with him helping with the newsletter and acting as the treasurer.

As I have become older I cannot do as much as I want to do for other people. I feel badly about this because I feel I am not making an adequate contribution to society. Logically, I know people can only give what they can and nobody can judge the effect of what they do. I am very aware that people are influenced by the way we act and behave, yet we may never know the influence we have on others. In some cases we are not meant to know and we would not gain anything by knowing. All we can do is our best whether we like it or not and leave the rest to God. The reason I am saying this is that I am now beginning to see that one of the ways it seems I can help other people is through my writing. I can let the world know that a severe disability is not the end and that it can be turned into something positive. I always believe in the saying, 'As one door shuts another opens'; God works through the opening and shutting of doors. I am sure that my apostolate to people and especially to disabled people will go on throughout my life.

Have-A-Go Club

I have described the Saturday Venture Clubs but my real baby was the Have-A-Go Club and this started round about 1974. This idea arose because I became concerned about children who were disabled and did not have anywhere to go in the school holidays and did not meet with children who were not disabled apart from their own brothers and sisters. I had the idea to form a holiday club for such children. I remember suggesting to Jackie that it could be called 'Have-A-Go' Club. She agreed, and for two or three years helped me to get it going. Then she said, 'Over to you, Liz!'

The main reason I wanted the club to be called 'Have-A-Go' was to encourage the children literally to 'have a go' in whatever way they could. We covered all kinds of youth club activities, went swimming each week and twice a week went off on different outings. ILEA supported and encouraged us, gave us money and two buses. Mick became my co-leader and managed to get the Sarah Siddons Youth Centre to help us with staff and run some of the activities for me. We made a good team.

Fund-raising was a big job as we still needed a lot of money. I made contact with various charities like Westminster Amalgamated Charities, Scope and a number of others. Looking back I feel the club had a good name with the different charities I used to approach, and social services were always contacting me to see if we could take another child. I am still in contact with a few of the children and their families. I have lost count of the number of children who have passed through it. Some of them are now married and have good jobs. Others are sadly too disabled to work.

The parents also benefited from the club; it gave them a welcome break and a chance to do other things, perhaps with the rest of their families. We also welcomed the other children of the families. The parents used to come and they liked to have a non-professional ear to listen to them and the opportunity to talk over their problems. I often found myself in this role. This was fine, but I always said the children came first and that we were not just baby sitters. Having a go was the object of the exercise.

When the children came back year after year, one could see a change in them. Some of them had improved physically, some had grown up and others always seemed to stay the same but I loved them all.

When ILEA was disbanded I very sadly lost Mick as well as the people who had been supporting me from ILEA. Westminster City Council took over the main bulk of the financial side of supporting the club. When they first came to see me about the club they definitely wanted me to carry on and to find some other people to run it with me. They agreed that I could advertise in the local paper. We interviewed about eight people and I managed to get six people whom I felt happy working with.

One of the things I didn't like about this new arrangement was that the staff at Westminster City Council did not seem to understand the difference between physically disabled children and children with learning difficulties, or emotional or other special needs. Another problem that arose was that the youth officer did not find it easy to communicate with me and on occasions avoided me. I had to find transport for the club members from local churches, which caused a great deal of extra hassle. I had to train the staff about the different disabilities, and what they could expect from each child.

Although I loved running the club, after working like this for two years I felt I had been doing it for long enough and wanted to resign. I told the people concerned that I would run the club for one more year and then I was going to give up. I remember their first reaction was to ask who would take over. I said, 'That's your problem. I'm sure you will find someone.' At the back of my mind was the feeling that if the club was centred around me I had not achieved anything for the integration of disabled children. As I was telling them this I was having a hard time trying not to get emotional. I felt I was giving away my little baby and it hurt for a very long time. However, I knew it had to be done.

After the end of the next year's summer project I wrote and told the parents that I would not be running the club any more but that I was sure that it would still go on. I am pleased to say that was three years ago and the club is still running.

Reflection

Thinking about founding and running clubs and groups and maintaining their life through major changes, it is also important to remember that although one begins something it should not depend on one person entirely. There must be room for others to come in and help it grow in different directions. I think God was with me when I made the decision to withdraw from the Have-A-Go Club because I was in hospital when the project was being run the following year. If I had not handed over, many parents and children would have been hurt. From this I learned that you must know when to let go.

On giving up the Have-A-Go Club I realised how fond I was of children and it pained me deeply to acknowledge that I would never have children of my own. The fact that I have committed myself to celibacy does not take away the love and affection I have for children. For about a year I had to work through feeling torn between the commitment I had made and the desire for children in spite of the fact that it was physically out of the question. I had to channel my energies in another direction to help me come to terms with the situation.

6

Vincent

My concern for other disabled people probably stems not only from being disabled myself, but also from having a brother who was disabled. My favourite brother, Vincent, was born in 1950. It soon became apparent that he had hydrocephalus. Vincent was born with too much fluid on the brain which made him have a large head. But he did not really look too much out of the ordinary compared to some children who have this problem. Vincent as a child was not too physically disabled; he was slow in his movements and his co-ordination was affected.

With the Family

I cannot remember much about Vincent's early years because I was away in Pinner. However, when Vincent was three, we went to Lourdes together. We stayed in the hospital and my mother used to push us both around in big old-fashioned wheelchairs. I remember when the priest came round with Holy Communion, Vincent stuck his tongue out and received the sacrament though he had not yet made his first communion. It was no good saying 'No' to him, he knew what to do. My mother was kneeling behind our chairs and it was all over before she could do anything about it. There were no flies on Vincent!

When I came home for the holidays, Vincent and I used to play. We played on the floor because it was hard for me to stand up. I felt safer on the floor. Vincent, somewhat boisterously, would knock me about and Mother would give him a slap on the leg to calm him down. I did not help because all I could do was laugh.

Sometimes Father would take us to the heath to play ball – piggy in the middle, if I remember correctly. Vincent would try to play with my other brothers and sisters while I sat in my chair and watched. Father would come and sit down beside me and tell me a story about a nightingale.

I remember one Christmas Vincent asked me to help him wrap up his presents. It was the blind leading the blind. At one point, I asked him who the present was for; innocently he replied, 'For you!'

It was hard for Vincent to entertain himself or join in our games because he just couldn't concentrate. So Vincent fell in love with buses. I think he knew every bus number in our district. He used to get a Red Rover ticket and go off everywhere. Our parents must have lived on tenterhooks when he went off and they just had to wait for his return.

One day my sister, Clare, took us for a walk alongside the woods. I was in my wheelchair and Vincent came too. A man came up and asked Vincent the way to some place or other and Vincent proceeded to tell him how to get there. Clare could see this man was dangerous and I can still see her grabbing Vincent's hand and pushing me, running home as fast as she could to tell Mother what had happened. She was petrified. Vincent learned not to talk to strangers!

Vincent went to the local primary school until he went to a special school for disabled children in Plumstead. He was collected each morning. He had a favourite teacher and I think the liking was mutual – he was her favourite pupil. To this day she sends my parents a Christmas card. When Vincent was twelve he was sent to a boarding-school in Godalming in Surrey run by the Sisters of Mercy. I think he was reasonably happy there.

While he was at boarding-school he went to the cinema with some of the boys. As he was coming out he stumbled, and his companions called to him, 'Look where you're going!' Vincent replied, 'I can't see.' Back at school he was put to bed and one of the staff contacted my parents to say Vincent was not well. My father went straight down to see what was going on. He left Vincent at school and returned home devastated. I shall never forget the look on his face. My mother, in her calm, matter-of-fact voice said, 'I am sure Paul will take us there by car.' He did and then they took Vincent to Great Ormond Street Hospital for Sick Children.

At this point nobody knew why Vincent could not see. I remember thinking, 'My favourite brother can't see! Why? Why didn't the school tell us?' I was cross and hurt, but I had to keep it all to myself for the sake of my parents.

It turned out that Vincent was suffering from meningitis. He had a further attack which damaged his brain. Before that later attack he could communicate with the family. He could remember the past very clearly and he wrote to every single person he knew, some of whom we ourselves had forgotten, as if to say, 'Goodbye! This is it!'

I used to go and see him when he was in hospital in Maida Vale. For about three or four months he was very seriously ill indeed, and on a number of occasions it was touch and go whether he would pull through. In our parish, prayers were said for him every Sunday morning.

After he had been at Maida Vale for five or six months it

was obvious that somewhere more permanent had to be found for him. In the end he went to St Lawrence's, Caterham, which is a large institution for those with severe learning difficulties. This was chosen mainly because it was near to our home. It must have broken my parents' hearts to have to take him there as it broke mine every time I went to visit him. There were about four staff for every twenty-five or thirty patients.

Initially, Vincent came home every weekend. When he came home, bearing in mind that he was blind, he had to sleep in my parents' bedroom. I often recall, with love, hearing Father talk to him as he gave him a wash or took him to the toilet. Vincent always knew when he wanted to go to the toilet. He still had his dignity. He would stand up to indicate he wanted to leave the room. Father would put his arm round his shoulders and they would go out. When it came to eating, Vincent always sat in the same place. There was nothing wrong with his appetite. He enjoyed his food.

Vincent also loved music. He followed Father's love of classical music but he also liked Gilbert and Sullivan. When Vincent came home from hospital at the weekend, my father would entertain him by putting on records of classical music. Vincent's favourite piece of music was Tchaikovsky's *1812 Overture*. He used to stand up and try to conduct it, especially when Father was there. I shared his love for the music of Gilbert and Sullivan. Music kept him happy for hours. At the hospital he tried to join the music group but he would not co-operate, so the group would not have him back. Was there a disagreement about classical music?

Vincent and I went to Lourdes a second time when he was eleven and I was fourteen. We stayed in a hotel this time, and one of the main things I remember about this trip to Lourdes was that somebody allowed Vincent to go to the baths and there he had a fit. The person who was looking after him had to walk him round and round to settle him. I didn't understand, but being the big sister I told him to pull himself together and behave himself. It wasn't till afterwards that I realised what had happened. As a result of that incident the Handicapped Children's Pilgrimage Trust made it a policy not to allow children prone to epileptic fits to go into the baths.

In 1981, Father Michael Garvey, who used to take mentally and physically disabled children and adults to Lourdes each year, agreed to take Vincent and me to Lourdes with the Across pilgrimage. Since Vincent had been ill there had not been an opportunity to go to Lourdes. I was a bit reluctant to insist because I was not sure how he would fit in, bearing in mind that he was blind as well as having learning difficulties. I spoke to Father Michael about it and he said, 'Let's go and see him and I can make up my mind.' To my joy he agreed to take Vincent. The biggest problem was trying to get a passport organised. Vincent had difficulty in holding his head up because it was so heavy, so taking a photograph was going to be difficult. However, Father Michael sent somebody down from the school where he was headmaster and they managed to help Vincent to keep his head up while a photograph was taken.

Vincent was probably the most disabled person on the pilgrimage. When we arrived, one of the first things we did was to go to Mass. Vincent went to Holy Communion when he was able to at St Lawrence's. I was not sure how long it had been since he had received communion but I saw no reason why he shouldn't do so now. I explained this to Father Garvey and he agreed. I shall never forget it. Vincent swore all the way through Mass! He did not know what he was saying. He was simply repeating what he had picked up at St

Lawrence's during his sixteen years there. I pretended not to know him and kept apologising for him. Father Garvey told me not to worry. It was all right!

During that week, Vincent came out of his shell. Somebody told me that he had made the sign of the cross. He was in an environment of love where he was accepted as he was. We were always the last in the dining room – we took so long to eat – but nobody minded. We were given a lot of love that week. I wouldn't have missed it for the world.

St Lawrence's, Caterham

I often visited Vincent in hospital, sometimes with the family, sometimes with friends. Dr Therese Vanier came with me on occasions, and we would take Vincent to the canteen. Therese would go off and collect what we wanted to eat because we could not carry it. I never forget the dignity and respect she had for us in allowing us to pay for the tea. I was the hostess and she only did what I could not do. Later, a friend named Sue and Father Austin Garvey used to come and visit Vincent with me, but by that time he was completely bedridden and a touch on his face was the only way of evoking any kind of response. These were very sad days but I would not have missed them. To this day I am sure Vincent knew that we were there.

As I have already mentioned, Vincent went home at the weekend. Over the years I could see that it was becoming harder for my parents to cope with these visits. I talked about this once or twice with Therese Vanier. After a year of thinking about it we decided to go to see the social worker at the hospital. I remember Therese saying to me that if I changed my mind about going, even when she, Therese, arrived at my door, it was OK not to go.

Vincent

It was a very difficult decision but I did go to see the social worker. She thought I was in a wheelchair and booked the board room for the interview because it was on the ground floor. She was amazed that I could walk. Therese made it quite clear right from the start that she had not come to do the talking but only to interpret. I explained that I was concerned about the strain my parents were under, having Vincent at home at fortnightly intervals. The social worker said that I had opened the door, because although they like families to show an interest and it was good that my parents did, the hospital felt that it was not good for Vincent to be moved from his environment. It disturbed and unsettled him. They were reluctant to say anything because not many people in the hospital had visitors or went home at weekends. I said to her to pretend she hadn't seen me and to go and see my parents to discuss the matter with them.

She asked me if I wished to see Vincent. Of course I did – so we went to the ward. The ward was not expecting us and Vincent was sitting on the verandah in scruffy clothes and with his head down. I was heartbroken to see him looking so uncared for. I think what really happened was that the patients were dressed in any old clothes most days. They were only made to look smart when visitors were known to be coming. I left Vincent, feeling very unhappy about what I had seen. The social worker said that she knew it was very hard but she felt I had done the right thing and that she would let me know what happened when she had seen my parents.

I was very weepy all the way back in the car but there was little that one could say. It was very painful but I knew it was the right decision. Part of me felt I had gone behind my parents' backs but another part felt that something had to be done.

A few weeks later I went home and my parents told me that the social worker had been to see them and had explained that it would be better for Vincent if he did not come home at the weekends. I did not know where to look but my parents seemed to think it was the right decision. To this day they do not know that I had been to see the social worker. However, I have now told my sister, Mary.

In 1982, Pope John Paul II came to visit Britain. Vincent had been chosen to go with my mother from the Caterham parish to Southwark Cathedral. I had an invitation from the Westminster diocese. Unfortunately, Vincent was not well enough to make it on the day. I felt very sad because I would have loved to have met up with him on that special occasion.

In 1983, Vincent became very ill. In March he developed a chest infection and was moved to an intensive care unit. On 14th March, Vincent's birthday, I went home on my way to the hospital, as I had done for the last seventeen years. My mother wasn't there, and all I could get out of Father was that Vincent was not well and she was at the hospital with him. Father told me Vincent would not be able to eat the sweets I had selected for him. My sister, Felicity, arrived and got us organised including taking some food for Mother to eat. Felicity then told me that Vincent was dying and that it was only a matter of days. When I saw Vincent I realised how ill he was. Father and Vincent used to call me 'Throb'; would I ever hear Vincent call me that again? Father was trying to give him some water. At that time I had started using a teaspoon to eat with. I thought the same might help Vincent. I went off to the ward sister to borrow a teaspoon. It did help. Father responded, 'You clever clogs!' That was the last service I ever did for Vincent.

I had planned to go back to St Lawrence's on the Wednesday afternoon. However, my mother's instincts told her to be there by 8 a.m. Vincent died at 1.15 p.m. that afternoon. My mother called me from the hospital; she could not tell me what had happened but said that Paul would come and collect me. Paul told me that Vincent had died and we both cried. Paul also suggested a glass of sherry might help calm me. I told the warden who said that she thought it was for the best. I was angry at her insensitivity: I had just lost a brother whom I dearly loved and I did not want to hear a remark like that.

Paul and I went home to be with our parents and the rest of the family. The funeral was a week later. Father Michael and Father Austin Garvey and Father David Wilson came; they had supported me over the years and had visited Vincent over the eighteen years he had been in the hospital. Father Salmon, who was the parish priest at Purley, was the chief celebrant. I am not sure whether he had ever visited Vincent, and the parish had stopped praying for Vincent years ago. The chaplain of the hospital had given Vincent very little pastoral care apart from giving him the sacrament of the sick on a number of occasions. The ward sister attended the funeral, as did some of the patients.

Members of the family react in different ways to a disabled member. My sister, Mary, helped me to understand this when she asked me whether Vincent realised that she never went to visit him. She said she couldn't because it was too painful. I am sure that he did somehow and I told her not to worry. I understood exactly what she meant. What we have to remember is to try to understand and respect one another's feelings and to help each other to deal with a given situation in a variety of different ways.

Reflection

Vincent was put into a hospital for people with severe learning difficulties for eighteen years because there was nowhere else for him to go. My pain for Vincent was intolerable at the time, so I can only imagine what it must have been like for my parents. The hurt and the rejection they felt must have been unbelievable. This gave me a better insight into what other parents must go through in dealing with their children who are disabled. It also made me realise how little priests are trained to cope with families in this kind of situation.

7

My Own Flat

Possibility to Reality

In July 1981, the possibility emerged of a Peabody Trust flat in North Kensington being free. I was nervous, but I thought the least I could do would be to go and have a look. I remember talking to Meg, who was then the warden, who told me all about the rent, the laundry facilities and how independent I would have to be. This was a new venture for Peabody. To my knowledge Peabody had never before taken anybody as disabled as I was. My social worker, Jane, and I went to look at the flat. We walked round it and something inside me told me I should try. Jane felt it was right but I knew I would have to have assured back-up from the social services.

At this stage we had not approached the social services. There had to be a case conference about me. At that conference were the senior social worker, two local authority social workers, my own district nurse and the nurse from the northern area. I sat outside the door. I was told that the district nurse, who knew me well, said at one point, 'Why not call Liz in?' Their faces fell. They had imagined me to be much more disabled than I actually was and given the facts they had every right to think like that. I was beginning to find it hard to swallow; I was incontinent and using a catheter; and my voice was very weak.

They were surprised when I appeared. I had a list of questions. Perhaps they thought they were just going to manage me! The social worker from Scope thought that I could have a community care worker once a day and a home help five days a week. I agreed with this. However, it would be another two months before the flat would be available. If Mary, the warden of the hostel, accepted this, I would be all right. I came away from the conference with mixed feelings: feelings of dependency but also of freedom. I would give it a go!

I moved into my present flat on 30th November 1981. By coincidence, this was the Year of the Disabled. The community care and the home help began to function. My friends came to help me unpack. My mother came up on the Saturday to make sure everything was all right. On the whole I settled in very well. I loved it. It was mine! My own home! I could arrange it just as I liked. The warden at Peabody told me to be independent. This made me more determined than ever that I was not going to depend on her unless I had to. I must admit she was always kind and came whenever I really wanted her. The nurse visited twice a week.

Independence

Before I came to the flat I did not have to think where my food would come from. The milk was always delivered; it was not my concern to make sure it was there. Now I was in the flat I had to arrange for the milkman to deliver milk and I had to pay the bill each week. This also applied to the rest of my food. If I wanted to eat I had to make sure that the food was in the flat. The flat had to be kept clean, so again I had to see that cleaning materials were in the house so that my helpers could do the housework and I could do my little bit.

This all meant that with the money I received each week I had to pay the bills for water rates, phone, electricity and all the other expenses involved in running a home. My mother had always helped me to budget but now I had more responsibilities. I started to keep an account book to help me see where my money was going. Over the years I have found this system very helpful.

Having one's own key means one can come and go as one likes. I, like others, had to make sure I was at home to let expected visitors in, or to receive goods if I had arranged for them to be delivered. Becoming more independent changed my life a great deal. I had to plan my days in a much more orderly way, and not abuse my freedom.

There was a problem with the community care assistants. They were all young and not fully trained and seemed to know little about disability. They kept changing; I didn't know who would come next, and they did not appear to understand the problems I had regarding feeding. As time went by and my swallowing became more difficult, the assistant and I got more and more frustrated. I remember a lad of twenty-three telling me that, if I wanted to, I could feed myself with a spoon. This was precisely what I had been told not to do because it would increase my spasticity. One day he could not be bothered to put my food in a bowl. He fed me by the spoonful from the saucepan. I just felt all my dignity drain away. I tried to make a joke about it but underneath I was seething.

On another occasion, a community care worker came to give me my supper. We got on fine. I was due to go to a meeting at 8 p.m. My friend came to pick me up at ten to eight and I asked the care worker to finish the washing-up and pull the door to as he left. When I arrived back from the meeting at 10 p.m., David was still there, sitting in the chair, watching television. I asked him what the hell he was doing. All he could say was that he was not taking advantage of me. 'I wouldn't dream of hurting you.' I knew at this point that something was wrong. He was either drunk or had been taking drugs. I said goodnight to my friend, who wanted to make sure that all was well for me. When my friend had gone I made David a cup of coffee while I made a cup of tea for myself. I can still see myself giving the tea to David by mistake. All he could say was, 'You're not going to report me, are you?' I said, 'I don't know. I haven't decided.' I really didn't have any intention of reporting him. Later, I discovered that he had a bottle of vodka. No drugs! There was actually something very nice about David but I continued to play him along for about a week. He was really kind-hearted. Later, I heard he was in hospital.

Community Care

Although at the moment I have a very nice community care assistant, I am concerned about community care. It does worry me that such workers can go in and out of the homes of the disabled, especially when they are not trained. It is all very good for the government to encourage disabled people to live in the community, but this does require a lot of resources, including carers adequately trained to deal with different kinds of disability.

Having to accept personal help from others is very difficult. The least society can do is to keep in mind the dignity of the disabled person and how humiliating it can be to accept very personal help from another human being. Apart from exceptional cases, each disabled person along with the professionals should be involved in deciding how their individual needs can be met in the home.

I now receive the high rate of attendance allowance so I am able to employ somebody to come and help me twice a week for three hours. She does my housework and helps me in whatever ways I need. Paying for private help does give more leeway. Such a person can do things that social services may not allow their staff to do; for example, putting up curtains.

The nurses come in two or three times a week or whenever I need them. They always tell me to call them if the need arises and never make me feel a burden. We laugh and when they leave they say, 'You know where we are, call us if you want anything.' We often have a friendly chat when they have time for a coffee.

Friends in the Block

Over the ten years I have been here there have been three wardens. Our relationship has been good but with the first two I felt it never got further than them seeing me as a disabled person. This affected the other tenants in the block and they would talk down to me. Eighteen months ago Mary took over as warden. Not only do I get on well with Mary but she has helped the other tenants to realise that there is a lot more to me than being disabled. The tenants now treat me much more like a normal human being, which makes me happy and helps to increase my confidence. A couple of the tenants in the block became friends. Alf, the handyman, put up cupboards and did odd jobs for me. Two years ago he had a heart attack and died. He is missed by us all, not to mention his wife, Gladys.

Two and a half years ago Nell and Sid moved into the block. They had seen me around, going shopping and getting on the bus. They said I always looked as if I was about to fall over. On Tuesdays Nell and Sid used to play darts and I would go to watch them, I haven't the faintest idea about darts, but I would tease them telling them they were cheating; and they, in their turn, tried to 'wind me up' by saying they would come and sort me out.

Nell had a catalogue and she helped me to make some purchases for my flat. They also took me to the Co-op in Hammersmith to buy some furniture. On New Year's Day, because I belong to a ticket scheme called Shape, I was able to get tickets, at reduced cost to the disabled, for a concert which included the *1812 Overture* by Tchaikovsky. It was very enjoyable, but sadly this was the last time I went out with Nell and Sid.

Early this year Nell was in hospital and I went to see her with Sid. We were taken by their son. Two days later, I saw the ambulance taking Sid to hospital. I rushed out and as he struggled to breathe, he said, 'Bye Liz – see you!'

I never did see Sid again. He went to the same hospital where Nell was a patient, and he died a couple of days later. I was so shocked, all I could think of was poor Nell. Sadly, I could not go to the funeral because I was going to Lourdes, but Nell knew I would have been there with her, if it had been possible.

When I returned from Lourdes, I tried to give Nell as much support as I could. I think she is remarkable the way she has coped. We are great friends, and we talk about many things. I feel I can call on her when I need to or when I want to know how she is if I haven't seen her about.

Reflection

Since I have come to the flat, the role of the community care and home help workers has changed. Initially, the community carers did the more personal things, such as bathing, giving one a meal and making sure everything was safe, whereas the home help did the housework, and fetched one's shopping and pension. Now they have amalgamated and are called community care workers and they do all the jobs. This may not be so in all local authorities but this is how it is in mine.

I still feel there is a need to give community care workers more training to help them understand the needs of disabled people, and what it feels like to depend on others for personal help. Maybe one day I will write a book on this subject because I feel so strongly about it.

Two years ago the government launched a scheme for disabled people. Funded by local authorities, it is intended to enhance the independence of disabled people. All applicants have to be in receipt of the disability living allowance at either the middle or higher rate, and the disabled persons themselves have to be involved in organising how much care they need to receive.

So far I have not felt the need to look into this matter, but the day may come when I do. As long as the disabled person is not being looked after by a relative, they may apply for this grant. To find out more about such grants contact should be made with the local social services department.

8

Daring to Reveal Myself

A Sound Friend

I know I have already mentioned Father Austin Garvey. He gave me my first retreat, but I had no idea that he would become a lifelong friend. He said something very important to me when I was seventeen or eighteen. He said I will always have some of my problems, so why don't I use them to help other disabled people? That was one of the key pointers to a better life for me.

He went to Peru for twelve years, and when he came back in 1978 it was almost as if he had only been gone a short while. I remember going out for lunch with him, and there he was cutting my food up and telling me what was going on in Peru. He told me he would be going to St Patrick's in Soho and said I could go and visit him sometimes so we could talk about things. For the last fifteen years I have been going to see him most Wednesdays. Sometimes I just tell him how things are, and at other times I ask him for advice or just chat.

Father Austin has seen my disability increase over the years and he has given me no end of support in trying to come to terms with it. Once I was asked to write an article about prayer and the disabled and he gave me great encouragement.

Every Friday night, Father Austin holds a service called the

'Stations of the Cross' and I try to go whenever I can. The Stations of the Cross are a form of worship to help us think about the passion of Christ and remind us that he died to save mankind from sin. For me, and for many others, it is helpful to see how we can take up our cross and follow Christ.

Father Austin has always treated me as an equal and would never talk down to me. If I say something or ask him a question he will always give it a great deal of thought before he answers, and nine times out of ten what he says has always given me a lift and helped me see things in a new way.

Sometimes he may not say much but I am very aware that he has felt for me when I have been going through a painful patch. Whenever I have been in hospital, he has always made an effort to come and see me.

Once when I was on a retreat he was giving, I was having breakfast in my room and it suddenly hit me that everyone else was downstairs enjoying a nice cooked breakfast and the tears started. This was not the time for tears. I had a meeting in ten minutes. Somehow I managed to put a brave face on and get through the meeting without anyone realising how I was feeling. At coffee time I was still feeling a bit choked. I caught Father Austin's eye and told him what was going on inside me. He thanked me for being able to tell him, and reminded me it was a good witness to others, meaning that yes, it was hurting, but I was still carrying on. I felt encouraged when I was giving myself my next feed alone. A different person.

In the last two or three years I have been conscious that he has become busier, so I suggested to him that perhaps I shouldn't see him every week so that he would have a bit more time. I think he was grateful for this comment, but at the same time he made it quite clear that if anything cropped up he is always there. This is an example of how relationships can change, and it is a give and take situation. I always feel that Father Austin has given me more than he will ever realise, and certainly more than I have given him.

The Grail

In the early seventies I needed a holiday and a friend of mine suggested I went to stay at the Grail. The Grail is a secular institute for Roman Catholic women which does a great deal of work encouraging lay people to find out how God has gifted them and what work God is calling them to. There are three main forms of membership: Grail partners, Grail companions and staff members who live at the Grail centre as a community. I enjoyed my stay at the Grail very much and often go back. They make me more than welcome and look after me very well.

I have seen many changes at the Grail. It does try to move with the times and is continually trying to help people understand the changes in the church since Vatican II. I feel the Grail has given me a lot and has influenced me a great deal. In saying that, however, the Grail has never taken over my life. That is the last thing they would want to do. The Grail want people to become the people God has created them to be. I did try to see if the Grail companion's way of life was for me. In the end I decided it was not. Rather than separating me from the Grail, this decision brought me closer to it.

Ruth, a staff member of the Grail, helped me as a counsellor. We were chatting one day in the kitchen and she told me it might help me to have a counsellor to whom I could talk freely. Ruth suggested I had a think about this. The next time I saw her she asked me if I had given it any more thought and I said I had but I didn't know how to go about it. She smiled and said if I was willing she was too. I was so pleased as I already knew I could confide in her. We agreed to meet once a fortnight and if the need arose I could ring once in the week when we did not meet.

One day when we were talking about God I said that I thought it was God's will that I should be disabled. That was what I had been told all my life. Ruth was somewhat alarmed and told me quite firmly that God did not want me to suffer. In a strange way I did not think of my disability as a form of suffering. I did not know any other kind of life, but I believed that God had made me that way for a purpose. It was only as I grew older that, as people talked to me, I began to understand that I was suffering because I was disabled. I know I rebelled as a teenager, but I don't think I connected my rebellion with suffering.

When Ruth told me that God did not want me to suffer, I felt that the whole of what I believed in and the way in which I made sense of my disability had been taken away from me. I wept.

Ruth said to me, 'Liz, I can't go back on my words. You may not want to go on coming to me in a counselling situation any more.' I am sure I felt more pain at that time than at any other moment in my life. However, it was a turning-point. It was as if I had been shaken up; it made me grow up and think what a loving God meant. Until then, I had a childish relationship with God regarding this aspect of being disabled. Here was a chance for it to change. Now my idea of a loving God meant God revealing himself to me at a level I was mature enough to take on board. A loving God does not want people to suffer. Suffering is a mystery that we do not understand and I certainly don't; but one thing I have no doubt about is that, in a way that I do not understand, it can draw people to Christ and it can bring about God's kingdom.

I can still remember talking this over with Ruth when I had recovered from my upset.

My life was not wasted. I could use my disability to promote God's kingdom in whatever way seemed right at different times. That was a very deep experience! I learned later that Ruth was heartbroken and shocked at what had occurred between us. She must have been, because I shared so much of myself with her in the deepest confidence.

One day we were rejoicing because it seemed that the chiropractor was going to help me and take all the pain out of my neck. Ruth was there. 'Good', she said in a distant kind of way. The next time I saw her on my own, I said to her, 'What have I done? Are you happy about me going to the chiropractor?' She answered, 'Liz, I didn't know what you were thinking deep down, and I wanted to leave you free to be able to say exactly what you felt, just as when you come to see me.' I was always amazed at her astuteness and delicacy. I learned a great deal from that experience and sure enough the chiropractor helped but did not resolve my neck pain.

In 1980, Ruth died of cancer, and I missed her a great deal for a long time. When I wanted some advice I would often think back to what she might have said and often found the answer within myself.

Ruth knew I was fond of children and she encouraged me to take a course in religious education for children. She did not feel I would be able to teach, but she felt very strongly that I would be able to write a book to help parents and catechists when they had disabled children coming to their catechism class in the parish. The book has not been published but I am hoping it will be one day.

I still go to the Grail when they can find a slot for me to stay. I believe I get on well with them all. However, I feel closer to Jackie, Felicity, Liz and Betty. When I go there I spend time reading, writing and taking the opportunity to rest. One thing I like about the Grail is that I always know who to go to if I need help. When I am not in my own environment it is not always easy to do everyday things like making tea but there is always someone to give me a hand. I like to spend time in the chapel which is very peaceful and I can reflect and pray about life.

The members of the Grail are all getting older and it looks as though there will have to be some changes in their lifestyle and in the contribution they make to the life of the church. I am getting excited about how things will all work out.

Retreats

In 1978, when I first lost my voice, a great friend of mine suggested that I make a thirty-day retreat. At least I could put my enforced silence to good use and it might bring my voice back! Making such a retreat was a very big commitment. As I looked into it, the thought that it might help my voice was way down the list of priorities in trying to make up my mind. When I mentioned the voice thing to my speech therapist, she said it would not make any difference. So voice improvement did not come into my reasons for deciding to make this retreat.

In early November I set off for St Beuno's, situated near St Asaph, North Wales. I had sent my case on ahead as I would not be able to carry it myself. I wrote them a letter explaining what kind of help I would need. I needed an electric blanket, my food would have to be cut up for me and though I could manage stairs to a certain extent, a ground-floor room would be preferable. Apart from that, they knew little about me. All I knew was that I was about to make a retreat based on St

Ignatius' *Spiritual Exercises* and I knew very little about them; well, in fact, nothing! That's the way it should be! This gave one a real chance to trust in the Lord. If I now know someone going to make a retreat of this kind, I am careful as to how much I tell that person.

I was made more than welcome at St Beuno's. I had not been there long before Kathleen, who was going to look after me during the retreat, came to make herself known to me. We got on very well. I think she will always remember how she had to change my collar. The collar I was wearing had to be done up under my arms, and the part I attached to my chin was always getting food on it. This is why it needed to be changed so often. She hated doing it and we had many a laugh about it. In every other way I was treated as a normal retreatant. On the first repose day I was called 'Sister' by another person on retreat. I really had a shock when I realised I was the only lay person there. It was good to know that lay people were encouraged to make such retreats. Now many lay people do go to St Beuno's.

Patrick Purnell SJ was my director, who very gently but firmly led me through the *Exercises*. These *Exercises* of St Ignatius are a form of praying the Scriptures using your imagination; meditating on them slowly and maybe applying them to everyday life. We met each day for about half an hour to talk over the Scripture texts I had been given the day before and what had come up. I was having a bad patch with my voice but I shall never forget how Patrick, in a sensitive way, made sure he heard every word I said.

This retreat changed my life in many ways. I came to understand and love God in a new and different way. As I became in touch with my own feelings I was aware of God being at the centre of my being. I had wanted to change something in my life and up until that time I had not had the guts to set about doing it. I knew I had to; by the end of the retreat I felt I had the courage to go back and close the door on the previous chapter of my life. I remember Patrick telling me to wait a month before I carried out my decision.

I received many graces and blessings during that retreat. I know I tried to put all I could into it but I gained so much more than I gave. It might be of importance to mention that until I came, St Beuno's had very little contact with people with cerebral palsy. I was very struck that the allowances which were made for me were more concerned that I would get too tired than anything else, and in fact their worries were justified. I did get tired, but I would not have missed the opportunity. It was a great and wonderful experience.

I have returned a few times to make an eight-day retreat; once directed again by Patrick Purnell, on the other occasions by Father Michael Ivens SJ. All these retreats were different but each time I came to know the love of God in a deeper or different way. It seems good to recharge my batteries each year if I can, by going on retreat.

When I reflect on the retreats I have made, be they Ignatian or not, I realise that all occurred at times when I was facing increasing disability. First it was loss of voice when people had to be very close in order to hear what I was saying and the effort to make myself heard was painful; second, when I was having increasing problems with my bladder; and third, the long-drawn-out problems I had with swallowing.

Personal Commitment to Christ

Over the years while I have been making retreats, it has slowly come to me that somehow I want to dedicate my life to God. I know we become a member of the church if we are baptised, and if we are not old enough our sponsors make this commitment on our behalf at that time. Later on in life some people want to reaffirm their commitment. For instance, some people enter the priesthood or the religious life. However, I knew that wasn't for me. It wasn't what I was looking for.

What I sought was something to do with being disabled. I wanted to dedicate myself to God, by serving my fellow disabled people and wanting to be free to serve others in whatever way I could. Somehow in all that mess, prayer seemed to be the key but action when possible was also important. However, it was very difficult for me to formulate all this in words and to express what was going on deep inside me. I spent many hours pondering, praying and talking to Patrick. At times it was rather painful as I struggled to express myself to him. However, I knew I needed to seek his advice and guidance. Being a wise man he did not want me to rush into anything, and he challenged me quite a lot with what I was trying to say to him.

This is a very important process for anyone when they are trying to discern what Christ is asking of them. He knew I wanted to commit myself but the way did not seem clear. As always he was very sensitive when we talked about it, but it took us about three years to realise what it seemed that God wanted from me. In time it became clearer that God seemed to be asking me to commit myself to a life of prayer, poverty and celibacy, by the form of a vow. I did not want to commit myself to obedience. This was because nearly all my life I had been told what to do. The time had come in my own personal growth to take more responsibility for my own plans and actions. Of course I have to obey the laws of the country and church like everyone else, but in everyday events I decide what I am going to do instead of other people deciding for me. However, of more importance, my commitment is a private vow and not a public one, as it is if you enter a convent or monastery.

After prayer and reflection I finally managed, with Patrick's guidance, to get all this put together on paper in the form of a dedication. On 13th December 1983, I made my private commitment at the Grail. I'm sure there are many people who make private commitments to God, and all it involves is reinforcing their baptismal promises.

We had a lovely Mass at the Grail and I cherish the memory. Father Garvey and my friends Sue, Tony and Mary came. Tony is disabled and it was good to have somebody there who was also disabled. It was low-key, as I wished. I chose the hymn 'Come Holy Ghost', as I was asking the Spirit for his guidance and the prayer 'Take, Lord, and Receive' from the *Spiritual Exercises* of St Ignatius which made a great impact on me. This is one of my favourite prayers:

Take, Lord, and Receive

Take Lord, and receive all my liberty, my memory, my understanding, and my entire will, all that I have and possess. Thou hast given all to me. To Thee, O Lord, I return it. All is Thine, dispose of it wholly according to Thy will. Give me Thy love and Thy grace, for this is sufficient for me.

When you make a commitment, it can only develop and grow over the years. However, although you have committed yourself to celibacy, this does not stop you having sexual feelings towards people. There would be something wrong if this didn't happen. However, as long as you live by your commitment, this is all good and healthy and perfectly normal.

It is over ten years since I made this commitment. I have had one or two testing times, which have turned out to be growing-points, and looking back it has been a time of great grace. Celibacy is only one aspect of my commitment. One is always looking for ways for prayer to become an even more important element of one's life.

When I say poverty is part of my vow, I do not mean I am going to live without a roof over my head or make myself fast. No, I mean struggling to live and make the best of every situation, despite the limits that life imposes on me, as a disabled person. For example, there are limits on the way I can help others. I have a longing to go out and work in the Third World, but this is out of the question because of my own physical needs. My voice problem limits how much I can help others by speaking to them. I have been deprived of some good I would like to do for others. There are times in my life when it feels much more of a deprivation than it does at other times. A vow to poverty does not take away the disappointments; but it helps to enrich the kind of lifestyle I have to lead. I find this aspect of the commitment hard to explain because it has had different implications at various times of my life. I have ordinary human desires as well as a physical disability and all of these change all the time.

Counselling and Spiritual Direction

In about 1988 the Westminster, Kensington and Chelsea Disability Team, which consisted of a speech therapist, a physiotherapist and an occupational therapist, suggested that it might be helpful to me if I went for counselling. The reason for this was that they thought I had a lot of problems to cope with and it might benefit me to have a bit of extra support.

I was very reluctant to go for counselling because I felt it was a sign of failure, that I wasn't coping with life. Like a lot of people, I felt there was a stigma attached to it. I knew it would not be the same as going to my friend, Ruth. After humming and hawing about it in my own mind, I agreed to give it a try. Once I had realised that to accept such help was not a sign of failure and I was not going round the bend, I began to relax about going and to see the positive side of counselling. Going for counselling has allowed me to talk about things and work through some of my feelings, good and bad, and I am now a much freer person.

If I met somebody in the same situation, whilst understanding all their negative thoughts about counselling, I would encourage them to take the opportunity. There are centres which do specialise in helping people with disabilities and in some cases knowing this is a definite plus.

As I have mentioned, Patrick Purnell SJ gave me a long retreat in 1978. About a year later I asked Patrick if he would be my spiritual director. I think this came about because I knew there was something I wanted to do with my life and at that time it was not at all clear exactly what, but somehow I found I could confide in Patrick. People sometimes get panicky when they know you are going to a spiritual director. They think that you are being told what to do, or are going to become a nun or a priest. However, that hasn't been my experience with Patrick. Yes, we do talk about where God is in my life and what God might be saying to me, but Patrick mainly listens and tries to help me see things and will often help me see situations in a different way.

We have shared on a very deep level and I can't get away with anything with Patrick! He knows me too well. But more important, I wouldn't want to keep anything from him. I will never be able to put into words how much Patrick has helped me. As I have grown up, the relationship has changed and it has become more like a friendship. I know I can turn to him for advice or a listening ear when the need arises. He also knows that I will tell him off if he is overworking. I am aware he has helped many people, so I consider it a privilege that he always seems pleased to make time for me.

One may wonder why one has a counsellor as well as a spiritual director. Their work does overlap a bit, but they each see things from a different point of view. I suppose the best way to explain it is that the director tries to help you see where God is in your life and the counsellor is concerned with feelings but not necessarily on a spiritual level. Although both people might be aware that faith is an important part of your life, you would not always discuss this aspect with your counsellor.

Heythrop College

In 1988, I was staying at the Grail and I was talking about wanting to do something different with my life. Moira and I were talking about Heythrop College, where she had just completed a year's course in pastoral theology. As we talked, it occurred to me that this might be something that I could do, so I decided to apply to the college for an informal interview. When I met Father Theodore Davey, we talked about the course and a bit about my needs and he accepted me, subject to references. Like every other student I had to apply for a grant, and I was given an extra £750 for special equipment. Father Michael Ivors and Patrick Purnell acted as my referees.

I started the course in October 1988 and I went there three and a half days a week. We covered subjects such as Canon Law, the sacraments, theology and church and pastoral action, philosophy and many others. I was allowed to tape-record my lectures and in order to complete the course I had to do nine essays of about two thousand words each, as well as a dissertation. Every Wednesday we had a speaker who covered a subject concerning different aspects of pastoral care. We all had to take it in turns to look after the speaker. We also had to lead a seminar. I did mine on disability and got the rest of the class to experience what it felt like to be in a wheelchair or other forms of disability. I remember that it went down quite well, but I was worn out by the end of it.

My dissertation was about pastoral theology in the church and society for people who are disabled. I remember asking for extra time in order to complete it. This was granted although my tutor was a little sad that I wasn't able to complete the work within the year. I was pleased because I said I would need three more months and I was able to do it within this time.

I enjoyed my year at Heythrop and enjoyed being with people who had common interests. We believed in celebrating (including knocking back the wine!) and I often attempted to have a drink with them. I was accepted as Liz, and my standard of work was expected to be as good as anyone else's, and why not? However, allowances were made for my disability. For example, I had my own room where I could go to feed myself and they helped me to get transport to come home. I often return to Heythrop and it always brings back happy memories.

I had mixed reactions from people when I told them I was going to Heythrop, but on the whole people were very encouraging. Understandably, I think they were more concerned that I would get too tired, and in fact their worries were justified. I did get tired, but I would not have missed the opportunity. It was a great and wonderful year.

Reflection

Nowadays, many lay people are trained to direct retreats and do so. This is something I would love to do but having a speech defect makes this almost impossible. I have to accept the situation, and realise that this is one area in which I cannot help others. It would not be fair; people have enough to cope with during a retreat without the added burden of a director with a speech defect. Actually, I do not have the physical energy either.

Disabled people are quite as capable of directing as the able-bodied and I wish those who have influence in these matters would encourage them.

I enjoy going on retreat with my disabled friends. Today these are given at London Colney. These retreats take a very different form. They are informal and we learn from one another. There are generally two conferences a day and we are given plenty of time to get to know one another and for discussion among ourselves, as well as praying together. Because we are disabled we have to spend time helping one another. Presently, these retreats are run by two priests from Westminster diocese. It would be a good thing if more priests were to participate in this kind of work so that we could reach out to more people.

9

Physical Aspects of My Disability

Coping with Pain

Now I must spend a little time talking about physical pain. Some disabled people have no more pain than able-bodied people; for others it is a constant battle. I am not referring to childhood illnesses, we all have to endure those; nor the normal germs, headaches, bugs and toothache we get and can do something about. For somebody like myself, pain is an everyday occurrence. A woman I know constantly suffers from cramp in her leg. Another who has the same disability as myself suffers from bad back pain, due to the way she has had to sit all her life. I find it hard to admit that I am in that same category of having constant pain, not because I do not want to be associated with these people but because I know there are no easy answers.

When I was in my early twenties I was on a retreat. Quite out of the blue I had this pain which started in my neck and went down my right arm. I thought maybe I had been in a draught or I had caught a chill. On return from the retreat I went to the hospital and I was given a neck collar to wear. The doctor said I must have a trapped nerve, or perhaps the discs in my neck were rubbing together. At times the pain would go down both my arms and into my hands and all my fingers, and hence it was often hard for me to feel properly with my hands. I often needed support for my arms because they felt so heavy.

That was well over twenty years ago. I had no idea then that such pain was going to become part of my life. I never know when it is going to flare up. When I am in company I sometimes need a pillow or a cushion to give support to my arms or neck. Sometimes the pain is so bad that it makes me weep. Somehow the tears relieve the tension and I am able to cope again. The pain can be eased by traction, a mini-tens, heat and pain killers. A mini-tens is a small machine that sends electric impulses to a part of the body covered by a special patch, to block out pain. It is also worth trying alternative medicines. I'm prepared to try anything.

I have had traction on and off for many years. Over a year ago my doctors suggested it would be easier if I had traction either at home or in a hospital nearby. We decided it would be better if I had traction at home. I was worried about whether this would work out, because it would mean having traction applied sitting up instead of lying down. The physio at the hospital showed me a home traction kit. After thinking about it I decided to see if I could have the home kit on loan. The community physio manager persuaded the manufacturer to agree to this.

When the kit came it turned out to be even better than I expected, so I was very relieved. The community physio trained three people of my choice to be able to use the kit so that they can give me traction when I need it. I feel much more comfortable with this arrangement as I can say when I need it. It works out at once or twice a week at the most, and the pain is kept under better control.

My Bladder

The pain I have just described is due mainly to my disability. The other kind of pain that I experience may or may not be connected. In 1979 I lost control over my bladder. This may have been the result of my hysterectomy or it may have been because this just happens to some women. It is known that some people with cerebral palsy develop these kinds of problems as they grow older but, as far as I know, not usually to the same extent as has happened to me. I have been into hospital twenty-five times for my bladder problems, and in two different hospitals. Even with a catheter I kept leaking urine and had to wear pads. All kinds of techniques have been tried – for example, various injections to tone up the bladder muscle – but all to no avail.

Somehow or other I developed a fistula in my bladder. In fact the doctors admitted it was their fault. It happened in the course of treatment they had given me. Therefore in January 1982 I had a major operation to repair the fistula. Typically, I managed to have healing problems. I was in hospital for about five weeks, but even so this did not solve the leakage problem. Eventually I had my urethra closed and a supra-pubic catheter inserted. For eight years I had no more problems with my bladder. When I first went to this hospital as an in-patient, I typed out what I would need help with. The sister on the ward read it, and remarked that she could see we would get on like a house on fire. I can honestly say we did. We were always pulling each other's leg. At the same time she supported me in any decision that had to be made, and respected me as a human being who could be responsible for her own actions. She used to let me go out to church or to see the speech therapist if there was nothing going on concerning my treatment on that day.

In 1990 I began to get pain in my bladder again. I was given anti-spasmodic tablets, which a lot of people take, but they did not make a lot of difference to me. As with other people who take them, they gave me a dry mouth which added to my swallowing difficulties so I decided to do without them.

In May 1991, I went to see a consultant for examination, but nothing came of it except that I was sent home and told to go back to the anti-spasmodic tablets. I was cross and disappointed. I was no further forward. Eventually my own doctor asked me if I wanted a second opinion and sent me to the Institute of Urology. The consultant had me in for tests and within a week realised that I had two major problems. I had a little fistula in my urethra, and my bladder was contracted when it was filling up and this was the cause of the pain. He then told me that I needed two operations but these had to be done one at a time, as the second would depend on a successful result from the first.

In March 1992, I went into hospital to have the fistula in my urethra closed. This was meant to be a fairly straightforward operation and so it proved, but the after-effects were somewhat dramatic. I had two haemorrhages and had to go back to the operating theatre twice in twenty-four hours. I shall never forget the ward sister. She was very concerned on my behalf as she prepared me and didn't go home until I had returned to the ward. Father Garvey popped in to see me just as I was going down to the theatre. He gave me a blessing and said that he would be back the next day.

At two in the morning I began haemorrhaging again. I rang my bell to tell a nurse what was happening. She kept quite calm as another nurse called the doctor and the anaesthetist. I only got three doctors out of bed! I felt bad about this. They were a different team, but they said, 'What do you think we are here for?' Earlier I had remarked to the nurse that if she didn't like nursing she shouldn't be there. Later when I was feeling guilty about the trouble I was giving to the doctors she reminded me of my words. That put me in my place! She asked me if I wanted to contact anyone. I asked her to tell my brother Paul but not until seven in the morning. People couldn't have been more kind.

I don't think I realised how ill I had been until afterwards. I went down to the theatre and the next thing I was conscious of was being told that Paul had been telephoned and that he would be in later. I thanked them all in the theatre for what they had done and told them I wasn't coming back! When I returned to the ward all I can remember was people's kindness and concern.

I felt very weak. When Father Garvey came in again I told him I had been to the theatre. He replied that I had told him that the previous day. 'No,' I replied, 'I have been there again.' My parents had gone on holiday on the Sunday before any of this happened. Thank God they had already set off or they would never have gone. This is what I mean by a simple operation turning into a major drama.

I was not allowed to get out of bed for six days. It was very humiliating. I had to have everything done for me. I could not even pull myself up the bed. It was a good experience to learn at first-hand what some people have to suffer all their lives. When the consultant came round he told me to take things easy. 'We don't want you going back down again!' I was given about eight pints of blood but all the time I knew I was in good hands. This could have happened to anyone. Yes, I am disabled, but I am also prone to everyday problems.

In July of that year I went into hospital to have the second major operation to enlarge my bladder. This is quite a well-known operation but it is also quite unpleasant. I was in hospital for three weeks. Afterwards it was very painful to walk for about two weeks. I needed support to get me round the ward. As a result of this operation one makes a lot of mucus so my catheter kept blocking and I constantly had to have very unpleasant bladder wash-outs. It always seemed to happen when a visitor appeared, and explanation was rather embarrassing.

All the patients were in the same boat. One of the doctors had a thing about cranberry juice and how good it was for the bladder. We would encourage one another to drink it. To me they said, 'Well at least you can pour yours down your tube.' At last I had discovered an advantage in having a tube! (This is my gastrostomy tube about which I will tell in the next chapter.) I got on very well with the other patients. If one of them could not understand what I was saying, another helped. They told me to get out my 'foghorn', meaning the amplifier I use with my telephone.

One weekend, while I was in hospital, the ward closed and we were all transferred to another ward. Somehow, quite unconsciously, I had made up my mind that this was not going to work. The sister in charge of our ward took us up and explained our cases to the nurses who would be looking after us. About me she said, 'Liz can explain what she needs and when she needs help.' On the Saturday I wasn't feeling too well. I think the operation had some effect on my rib which I had cracked a few weeks earlier. I also knew I had another attack of mastitis. I knew what I needed were some painkillers and antibiotics but I could not get the nurses to understand my needs. My mother came and I was in agony. She wanted to intervene for me and I allowed her to do so. By that time I had a fever, and was at last believed. I was given antibiotics. I can remember feeling so frustrated because I was feeling so rotten on top of everything else. I tried to print out what I wanted on my communicator but the poor nurse could not make out what to do with the tape I had printed.

There was a further incident. I was having my teeth cleaned and I got told off for not spitting out. The nurse had no idea that I had a problem with spitting. I had to say, 'If you sit me up and put my bib on I might be able to do it.' In the end she did what I wanted. She said, 'You were right, weren't you?' I felt belittled because I had tried to put it kindly to her.

On the Sunday we were told that our own ward wanted us back. We couldn't wait to get back. We felt more at home there. The problems surrounding me had happened simply because the nurses had very little experience of disabled people. This happens quite often when I go into hospital, and I have to try to be patient and explain things so as to put staff at their ease. Most of the time it works but when it doesn't I tend to hit the roof and then come back to earth again.

Within about two weeks of my operation, my feeding pattern began to get back to normal but I had to work on it for about six weeks. During all that time I suffered pain but on the whole made a good recovery. One of the problems that did emerge was urine leakage around my catheter and at one time it looked as if the operation had not been a success. The last thing I wanted was to be humiliated by wetting myself and my clothes. It was a horrible feeling. However, it was just a question of having the right catheter, and the consultant managed to sort it out for me. For a little while I was scared that things were going to get worse but actually they have turned out to be much better.

One of the patients on the ward told me that she had trained herself to go without a drainage bag during the day. When I asked the doctor he said I could try this in my own time. It took me two and a half months to train myself. I am delighted to say that apart from the occasions when I go on long journeys or am not sure of the toilet facilities I may encounter, I can now manage without a drainage bag during the daytime, and that's after twelve years of wearing a bag. I feel very pleased with the outcome of the operation. The biggest bonus is that I am rid of the awful pain which I suffered for eighteen months which made me look worn and haggard. So pain can turn out to be positive.

I have had more than my fair share of trouble with my bladder. What hurt the most was all the humiliating moments I had from so many accidents due to leaking and not knowing when it was going to happen. On the whole people were very understanding, and that was a great help but it never took away how embarrassed I felt at times. I hope this is the end of my hospital stays for my bladder problems, although I am always going to have to visit the hospital for checks. It might be time-consuming but so far nothing has caused me to be alarmed.

Reflection

When all this was going on I did find myself asking God, 'When will it end? What have I done to deserve all this?' It felt as if my bladder was leading my life. I used to have days when I felt so depressed because I could not see any end to the problem. However, I just used to try and hang on till the feelings had passed. Looking back, I realise God was with me as I was struggling through it all.

A great deal can be done for people who have problems with the bladder and if anyone were to tell me they had a bladder problem I would advise them to go to their GP for referral to an expert urologist for the right kind of help and on-going management. Problems with the bladder are more common than most people realise.

10

Voice and Swallowing

A Predictable Voice

The part of my disability which causes me the most frustration is the way my speech and swallowing have been and are affected. This means that both communication through speech and socialising while having a meal are hard to carry out. However, onerous as these two problems are, their existence has also led to my meeting some terrific people and I do have better insight into other people's difficulties too.

As a baby, my speech was slow to develop and my mother did have her hands full trying to breast-feed and then give me a bottle as it was hard for me to suck. I think people felt I was just behind in developing – as is quite often the case with people with my physical problems – and that improvement would come in time.

At this time speech therapy was scarce. I first worked with the speech therapist during my last year at St Vincent's. We would work looking into a mirror but I cannot remember much more about it. I had to wear a plastic bib under my dress because I dribbled a great deal and the staff and my parents were worried in case I got a bad chest.

When I went on to school, the physiotherapist encouraged me by reminding me to swallow my saliva. I should have realised that I had a problem because I found it hard to do a dry swallow at night when trying to get off to sleep. Within six months my control over my saliva had improved no end, although I could slip back when I was tired, unwell or concentrating hard on something else, like writing or typing. Sometimes if my head is too far forward it still happens. I think I have mastered saliva control as much as I ever will.

Soon a speech therapist came to the school, and I can remember lying on the bed and doing breathing and tongue exercises. I did not like doing tongue exercises because they made my tongue hurt. She said that if it did not hurt I would not need to do it. One day when I was having feeding practice with the speech therapist I demanded to be shown how to eat with my lips together as my friends at school could, but without beating about the bush she told me this was something I would not be able to do. I felt cross. I wanted to be able to do this. My other friends could, so why not me? The fact that I spent part of the treatment time lying on the bed being helped to try to hold my lips together while trying to move my tongue about to a count of ten at that time seemed totally unrelated. I just didn't connect the treatment with my eating difficulties.

In the middle of the winter term, when I was fourteen, my voice suddenly disappeared. I would throw my arms about trying to get words out. I also developed a bit of a stutter, and pain in my diaphragm. The speech therapist helped me learn to whisper as I was putting too much effort into trying to talk. I also had to lie down after lunch in a relaxed position like mothers do when they are pregnant. I would much rather have gone to play.

The headmistress could not understand why this had happened. She tried to comfort me by telling me Our Lady must have gone about talking in a whisper. This didn't give me much comfort when all I wanted to do was make myself understood and I became very cross; it was just a silly idea she had. The psychiatrist was coming to school one Friday afternoon and I was told I had to go to see him. He seemed hard, but I remember him saying that if I relaxed I would get my voice back. The next time he came to school, my voice was much better.

At the end of the first term when my voice had gone, my parents had moved house. The speech therapist rang my parents to tell them about my voice loss, so they would know about it before I went home. I thought that was very kind of her. It had been hard when the girls at school made fun of my struggle to make myself heard and understood. At least my parents could explain to my brothers and sisters before I went home for the Christmas holidays.

I owe much to the speech therapist. She helped me gain the independence that other people take for granted. For instance, at the age of fifteen she helped me make my first telephone call. I was nervous as I did not think I would be understood but it was not as bad as I had thought it would be. Going shopping on my own was hard because people could not understand what I said. To practise shopping she would take me into town, write down what I wanted to say and let me get on with it, staying in the background in case I got into difficulty.

One day while we were out she offered me a cup of coffee. I refused because I knew I would have to ask for an extra empty cup into which we could pour half the coffee so that I would be able to hold the cup without spilling it. I felt too embarrassed about doing it. However, she said we were not going back to school till I had had a cup of coffee. 'You can do it, Liz. I'll pay, but you ask.' Finally I gave in and I asked for my cup of coffee and the empty cup. She carried it to the table and poured half into the empty cup for me. I was thrilled and she was very pleased. Another barrier had been overcome.

When I went back to work at the school, I went to see an ear, nose and throat (ENT) specialist. He couldn't examine my throat enough to see my vocal cords, but he told me I should stop trying so hard and learn to relax, which was easier said than done. I had a very quiet voice and found it hard to talk in a noisy environment. For instance, if I was helping the children in the dining room and wanted to say something to one of the staff, we had to go out of the room so that I could be heard. My voice loss lasted eighteen months but within three or four months after visiting the consultant I had made a full recovery and I and others thought the problem had gone for good.

I still had to ask people to write things down when I went shopping. If people had not met me before or had not seen me for some time, it took them a little while to get used to the way I spoke, but in general I just got on with it. I knew which sounds were hard for me to form and I would just have to think hard and take my time when I was trying to say them. I did in fact have about fifteen years of freedom until the next time.

Swallowing also didn't cause me any problems for some years. I was slow at eating and needed my food cut up. I made a mess but just made sure I wiped my mouth after a few mouthfuls. My mother used to put her finger to her mouth and I would know what she meant. As for drinking, most of the time I would use a mug and make sure it was not too full. When I went to Bristol the other people at the work centre used straws to drink and suggested I did the same. This did seem easier as it meant I didn't spill so much. I would still dribble at times which could be embarrassing, but

I would say 'Sorry' or 'Forgive me', and deal with it the best way I could.

All was well until Easter 1978 and then my voice started giving me problems again. One day I woke to find I had no voice – only a harsh whisper – and it was a strain to speak, let alone be heard. I was in the middle of running a club for disabled and able-bodied children and this was not the time to lose one's voice. We had a break-in at the club and I had to take the responsibility. I did wonder if this anxiety was why my voice disappeared. This is me all over. If I cannot find a reason why something has gone wrong, I tend to blame myself – a weakness I have had to struggle to overcome so many times. The club problem was sorted out and I regained confidence in running the club, but my voice did not return.

I struggled on for the next six weeks or so without quite knowing what to expect or what to do to help myself. I had forgotten all the hints that I had been given at school and became tired of people saying, 'I can't hear you.' 'What's happened to your voice?' I went to Lourdes in early May and Mrs Garvey, mother of the Garveys, who knew me well, kept giving me notepaper so I could write down the main words of what I wanted to say. When I returned from Lourdes the husband of the warden where I was living greeted me with the words, 'Have you got your voice back?' I felt like hitting him but I made a joke of it – but the answer was 'NO!'

I was referred to an ENT specialist who said I needed speech therapy. This was how I met Kate, my long-time speech therapist. We discussed what had happened, she examined me and gave me a few easy breathing- and voice-exercises. Easy for other people but very hard to me. She advised me to rest my voice as much as I could. I felt at ease with Kate the first time I met her, but I had no idea how long a struggle was ahead. However, this was the first time I felt I had someone who understood what my problem was all about.

I had not realised how much work is involved in the production of a single word. The diaphragm plays a large part in our breathing and ensures we have enough air to make sounds as our vocal cords come together. A few weeks after I had begun having speech therapy my vocal cords were examined. It turned out that I was probably using my false vocal cords. I didn't know we had two sets of cords until then. When I came back from theatre I was feeling sleepy, and when Kate came to look at my notes I looked up to see her there. She gave me a wave and a few minutes later she came over to my bed and said, 'It's important that you sleep now. We'll talk later.' Kate once again explained to me that I had to try to relax and not put so much effort into trying to get a voice. We had to work at trying to get me to produce a relaxed whisper.

I was older, and tried to put into practice what she helped me to do in therapy. My frustration was great at times, as I was sitting on committees and trying to run clubs. Making a phone call was hard work; it would wear me out at times. Very soon I was able to have my own phone with an amplifier. This made life easier but I still needed time to get comfortable and relaxed. If people don't know me it can still be hard for them to understand me and even for people who do know me, hearing me can be hard work. As I cannot write manually, Kate arranged for me to have a Canon communicator, which is like a mini-typewriter, so I can print out what I want to say when I go shopping or to meetings. When talking in a large group it can be very difficult to make myself heard. If I am sitting next to someone I don't know, I will ask them to read out what I have printed out on my communicator.

Perhaps I should explain that when I am told to relax, I do

not mean just sitting and reading a good book or going to a good show. The relaxation to which I refer is being able to relax my muscles, in order to let another set of muscles do the work. This is difficult to carry out. As well as relaxing, in order to make things work as well as they might, one has to get the timing right, which again is extremely difficult. Relaxation and timing also apply to my swallowing which I describe later. When I was at school, I didn't understand these principles. Now if people ask, I can try to explain or show them what Kate has put in my speech book.

My voice problem has never cleared up as it did when I was at school. I have good and bad patches, sometimes the bad ones last for weeks. This is something I have found very hard to deal with over the years, as it can make me feel insecure because I don't know what my voice will be like from one day to the next. In the past, I have been very depressed about it and have had to work very hard emotionally to try not to let this happen.

There are probably a number of reasons why I have bad patches. It could be tiredness, illness or physical pain. I may be worried or tense about something and that can throw my muscle tone out of action. Sometimes we cannot pin down a reason, it just happens. As there is no clear-cut answer I sometimes get all worked up and think the problem is psychological and I think it's my fault. This is not so at all. There are times when I fall down a lot; this is because my co-ordination goes. I don't blame myself for this or feel guilty because I fall down, so why should I get keyed up about my voice? Nobody else thinks it's psychological. Over the years Kate has given me a great deal of support and encouragement, and I think she deserves a medal for the way she has helped me handle my feelings. She has told me I have improved a great deal regarding this issue, and I know I have certainly worked at it over the years. I must confess that these types of feelings have come up in other aspects of my life but becoming aware of them makes them easier to control. I would just like to add that although Kate is a speech therapist, she has always shown concern and interest in other aspects of my disability.

One of the drawbacks about having a voice problem is that it limits what one can give to other people in terms of communication. Although I have trained to teach catechism and have experience in counselling, I am very limited in how I can put these skills into practice. I have given one or two talks but they have taken a great deal out of me, due to the effort I have to make to produce my voice. This is another reason why I feel my speech is one of the biggest aspects of my disability.

Swallowing Difficulties

In 1981, swallowing began to become a little harder. I mentioned it to Kate, and she suggested I had a drink of iced water before I had my meals to reduce the spasm in my tongue. This helped for a while, then the problem increased. One day I took my food from Meals on Wheels with me to speech therapy so that I could show her what was happening. I had already had an X-ray and the doctor told me my tongue was causing the problem.

I was by now living in my flat and having help with my meals from social services. Soon I had to have liquidised food from Meals on Wheels. These meals were never my favourite, but when you cannot cook it does mean you have one main meal a day, so it was better than nothing. In order to keep me as relaxed as possible I had to be spoonfed. I needed time to swallow between mouthfuls, and would get tired as it could take me up to forty-five minutes to have a meal. I would get different helpers from social services, and I found this very difficult as they never had time to understand the problems involved, and as soon as they did they would either leave or change their duties.

It was not long before I could only take liquidised food through a straw. I dreaded mealtimes because they took so long and I tired more easily. In 1986 I was at a summer school and felt so embarrassed that I was crying. I cried because I was feeling weak from hunger, so I tried to get a supplement drink down. I was sure in my own mind that things could not possibly get any worse but my hopes were in vain.

Suddenly it became harder and harder to swallow liquids. I just could not get the liquids from the front to the back of my mouth. I went to my doctor and showed her how I was drinking. She was horrified, and later confessed that it was one of the hardest days of all her working life. Kate also came to see me at home. As she tried to help me have a drink I asked her why I couldn't swallow. At that time she didn't know and as always she was honest with me and said so. I know she was very concerned.

I have never in my life felt so numb. I felt I was in a nightmare. Everyone panicked, trying to get me a bed in the hospital. I was aware of what was happening but I felt I had been transferred to cloud-cuckoo land. I knew what was going on but it did not feel as if it was really happening to me. It was as if it was a dream.

When I heard there was a bed for me in hospital that same day I did manage to pack my bag and get myself there. I rang my parents and told them I was going into hospital because it was hard for me to drink. I had told my sister Mary about my difficulties and made her promise not to tell my parents. I had no idea how serious my situation was.

When the doctor on the ward examined me, he told me I was as dehydrated as a camel in Africa. I was given a nasogastric drip. This is a tube that goes down your nose to your stomach via the back of your throat. It was horrible but at least it was getting food and fluid into me. Kate came to the ward the next day to see how things were going, as well as to give me a drink and show the nurses what to do. When the consultant came round he said that the main problem was my tongue and that I would have to find another way to get food into me. All I wanted to do was get under the bedclothes and cry; I felt so miserable. I could not take in what was happening. My family found it very hard to understand and it was not easy for us to talk about, because they were hurting too.

When I first lost the ablity to swallow liquids, I did not have pain from the effort of trying to drink. However, within a few months I began having pain following attempts to drink. We feel this is due to the effort I have to put into holding the liquid in my mouth before I can produce a swallow. The intensity of the pain can vary tremendously. Sometimes it lasts longer than at other times. I know it may seem a silly problem to have but, by Jove, it is real. Now and again it makes me cry. However, placing a heat pad around my mouth helps to relax the muscles, and sometimes I take an extra anti-spasmodic tablet to relieve the pain.

On some occasions I need to have a break from trying to drink. This seems to help break the pattern of the tension and pain building up more than it really has to. I can take extra liquid like fruit juice and water via my gastrostomy tube if I feel dry or I can suck a few mouthfuls of ice to keep my mouth moist. This pain occasionally occurs when I am talking, but it is more usually related to the effort of swallowing.

Because of the way I swallow, I tend to select who I'm

going to try and eat with. When I am with the family I just do what I can. When we have parties one of the family will help me with spoonfeeding. Sometimes if I have some alcohol I can get more down, but I soon get tired and will then go away and have a feed by gastrostomy. If someone sets me up, I am OK and can get on with it. Sometimes Mary, my sister, and I like to have a chinwag to catch up on each other's news, so she offers to help me and we kill two birds with one stone. Two things I am able to eat easily are meringue and avocado. When we do have family parties, most times my sisters make sure these are on the menu.

When people come to see me I like to offer them a meal even if I am unable to eat it myself. Over the years my parents have often had a meal when visiting me. If a friend is coming I will offer them a meal and say, 'I buy it, you cook it.' To start with this compromise was uncomfortable but I want to keep my friends, so I soon learned to handle my feelings and make them as welcome as anyone does when friends come to visit.

I sometimes go to stay at a lay community at Pinner in Middlesex. At mealtimes I join them and just have a little of whatever I like and someone will feed me if I want them to. They have known me for years and have seen the different stages as my swallowing has become a problem. When I first went to Pinner all they had to do was to cut up my food and make sure my mug of tea was within reach. I feel as comfortable as one can, given my situation, and they always make sure I have my feed before or after their mealtimes.

I know it is very hard for some of my friends, who have had to watch my struggle to try to eat. Although no one really liked the idea of my having a tube, over the years they have told me they are relieved to know that I am now able to manage to have enough food inside me without all the physical struggle I was having to cope with. It was a big price to pay to gain liberation from the struggle to have enough food to keep going.

Reflection

Nowadays much more is known about swallowing problems. In many cases, video-fluoroscopy is carried out with the speech therapist which can give a clear picture of what happens during swallowing. In most cases this means that treatment can be better designed to help the individual person to eat and drink. Speech therapists are more aware of swallowing problems and how to treat them, and nurses working in hospitals work with the speech therapists where possible.

The speech therapist has played an important part in my life due to my voice and swallowing problems. I have had about five therapists in total, two long term and the other three for much shorter periods. Also I was not having major problems with my speech at the times when the three were treating me. This was when I was at the work centre for people with cerebral palsy and my problems were minor compared with those of some of the others at the centre.

I think it is very important for people to understand that in some cases, as in mine, the therapist, no matter how good, cannot teach you to speak, have a good voice or swallow properly if you do not have normal function there to start with. However, the therapists who have worked with me have been able to help me make the best use of the abilities I have had at that particular time.

Kate has worked with me the longest and most recently so she has seen me through many ups and downs regarding my voice and swallowing. Each time I have a change in the pattern of what I can or cannot do we have been able to vary the treatment. Now and again it may just be riding it through until my muscle tone has settled, or we may have to find another way to tackle the problem at that particular time. Sometimes ice can help me speak and swallow better, another time lying down makes it easier to talk. So as my pattern of ability has changed over the years, Kate has helped me to maintain what I have left.

Other people do go up and down with their problems, and progress can vary. Some people can and do make a full recovery. As one who has benefited over the years from the help of the speech therapist, I always feel that the layperson does not really understand what is involved in being a speech therapist, and maybe they are not always given due credit for the painstaking work and care they give. I will always feel particularly indebted to Kate as a therapist and friend.

As I feel that speech therapists do not receive as much praise and credit as they should from the public and society in general, I try to make a habit of giving them support whenever the opportunity arises.

11

Feeding and Nutrition

Gastrostomy

The psychological side of living with a gastrostomy caused me a lot of distress, which I had to work through slowly. I will share some of this as it may be helpful to others to know that it is a normal reaction. However, it is a difficult transition and hard to see or take in at the time.

At New Year 1986, I was thanking God for all the good things that had happened during the year that was ending. Suddenly, I was thanking God that I was feeling stronger because I could get more food into me; at the same time I realised it was the presence of the tube which had brought this about and I had a good weep. I hated it. I was visiting Father Garvey in Soho, and went back to the house to join his other visitors. He could see I was unhappy and when we found the chance we slipped away so I could talk to him. I started weeping again and all I could say was, 'I hate the tube' and he gently encouraged me to have a good weep. When I had finished he said, 'Do you feel better now?' and I said, 'Yes, much', and I joined in with everyone else as if nothing had happened. This was the beginning of my coming to terms with my new situation, but a few more dark times still had to be worked through.

I had trouble with the tube coming out. When all this trouble was going on, my thoughts, I must admit, turned to suicide. Then I felt so guilty about having such thoughts, I kept them to myself. I just used to feel I could not go on living in this situation, it was too much to bear.

On one occasion I shared these feelings with Patrick Purnell. He listened sympathetically but confessed his own helplessness. I can still remember him saying, 'It's all right, Liz. It's a natural response but I know you won't do anything like that.' He was quite right. I wouldn't commit suicide because I know it would hurt too many people and deep down I know I can get through most things. However, it is a horrible feeling to have and very frightening. Feelings – maybe not as strong as this – arose a few times but with time they have become less as my way of feeding has become more natural to me. But now I will share why these feelings of suicide arose.

My reaction to losing the ability to swallow was not all negative; it created a great deal of emotional energy which I felt I could use to help others and stop me feeling bitter. No one thought I was bitter but I worried lest I became so. I decided to write a book about the Stations of the Cross to help me deal with my deep disappointment. The book was published in 1989 by St Paul's Publications, and has sold quite well. Even if it has just helped a few people it is worth it. I asked David Alton, MP, to write the foreword because I know he has a great deal of time for disabled people. He is against abortion of every kind, including children who are going to be born disabled.

To return to my struggle with the tube: once the tube was in place I thought that was that – all I had to do was get used to living and coping with it. But reality was not quite like that as for four and a half years I struggled with a variety of problems.

For example, the tube fell out sometimes; or the tube slipped into the duodenum, causing excess bile which made me feel sick. The remedy seemed to be to withdraw the balloon that goes with the tube a little. This worked for about two days and then I was back to square one. The tube needed changing but nobody wanted to do it, and this distressed me a great deal. I would go to the casualty department at the hospital but was told I couldn't keep going there. I was told my GP should change the tube. As good as she was, she had no experience in this technique and didn't feel she could take it on. The consultant said I could go to the ward. This was unsatisfactory as I had to wait for a long time and the nurses were not always very helpful and even suggested I might be removing the tube on purpose. On occasion they were impatient because of my speech. They couldn't understand me, so I asked the speech therapist to write a note, but this made little difference. Finally, I was to see the consultant to get the problem sorted out.

I had another idea. I asked the consultant if I could try changing the tube myself. I asked for two attempts on the ward to see if I was able. He agreed. I knew it would be tricky for me with my wobbly hand co-ordination, but I was over the moon when I realised I could do it. Kate contacted the consultant to make sure that if I was having a bad day I could go to the ward. This I felt was important as it gave me extra confidence but to this day I have not had to go back. Although I was more confident, this was not the end of problems with the tube. It still kept coming out. I wrote to the makers of the catheter for some hints on tube management, only to find that my tube was not of the correct type for gastrostomy feeding. I made quite sure I had an appropriate tube thereafter.

The site of the tube became very sore and I saw the stoma care nurse, Barbara. She was not sure she could help me over and above the advice she had already given me. The soreness was getting worse, and walking was most uncomfortable. I was at my wits' end to know what to do. Then one day I had a brainwave and wrote to the hospital for disabled people – the Royal Hospital and Home, Putney. I gave Barbara a copy of my letter and very soon we had a reply from the sister who ran the ward where nearly everyone has a gastrostomy, inviting us to visit. Maybe at last a solution was in sight.

We went to see the sister at Putney. She suggested I change my tube to a Conpak gastrostomy tube. It was hard to believe there really was a tube made specifically for feeding which my medical team did not appear to know about. She also suggested I had a holder to secure my tube against the skin of my tummy to stop it moving about. Barbara managed to obtain these items for me with the hospital consultant's backing. Life was easier, but my tube continued to leak and my skin was still very sore. Barbara tried everything she could to stop the leaking and the soreness, and finally I wore a small drainage bag to prevent my skin becoming excoriated by the leakage.

I felt that the tube should be moved as we seemed to have reached an impasse situation and the discomfort was really getting me down. I mentioned this to Barbara but she discouraged me from thinking this way because she knew it would be difficult for the old hole – the entrance for the previous tube – to heal, and I would then have two holes to contend with. As a stoma care nurse, she has a great deal of experience of problems of this kind, and will not build expectations unrealistically, giving patients false hopes. It cannot be easy for her to handle such situations but she is being truthful and I am full of admiration for the way she deals with them.

My skin became even worse due to the leakage and there

was little choice but to resite the tube. Even then, the doctors were unsure what would happen with the site of the former tube. They were right to be concerned because it has taken much longer to heal than I thought possible and in fact I eventually had a small operation to close the old entrance. However, it was worth it to have a new resited tube in a better position. It is now comfortable and much easier for me to manage. Barbara changes the gastrostomy tube every three months and the water in the balloon each week to ensure that the tube remains in place. She has been so supportive since we began trying to sort this problem out. I don't think she had ever worked with a client with cerebral palsy before but right from the start she always considered my full disability. She has been very professional and a good friend. She said I have helped her, but that is nothing compared to the help she has given me.

Having to feed by tube is a great social handicap. Every time I go out for any length of time I have to take my food with me and make sure there is a suitable place for me to feed myself as I need privacy. However, over the years I have become more confident and ask for a room, and most people just help me set up and leave me to get on with it, which is what I would wish. As long as I know I can ask for help if the need arises, I am fine.

Chest Infection

At Christmas 1988, I developed a cold that soon went on to my chest. This made me develop a cough which was worse when I tried to drink. I was at home with my family and anxious to get back to London to see the doctor so that I could get some antibiotics. However, I was not well enough to make it to the surgery so the doctor came to see me. He told me I had pneumonia and needed to be admitted to hospital.

I went into hospital for a few days. My chest X-ray showed that liquid I had been drinking had gone into my lungs and had caused the pneumonia. The staff on the ward just told me to be careful when I was trying to drink. I don't think they realised what was involved in my own particular swallowing problem.

After I had left hospital, I phoned Kate and I told her about inhaling when I was drinking. I did not fully understand how serious this was. She was coming to see me at home the next day before she went on leave, so said we would talk about it then. When she came I offered her a cup of tea and asked if I could have one. She shook her head and smiled, saying 'No, not with your chest.' I needed to find out what Kate really meant. She gently explained to me that because I was inhaling some of my drinks and had a chest infection, it was not safe for me to go on taking anything orally for the time being. My emotions were very mixed. It was hard to take in what she was saying. Did it really mean I could not try to eat or drink? Yes, it did for a while.

I knew Kate had been working all day and it would be some time before she got her evening meal. Therefore, I offered her a banana – others had to go on eating even if I could not. However, she declined and said, 'Let's put it out of sight.' I did not think I would be seeing Kate again for some time as she was about to go on leave, and I tried not to get upset by this new turn of events.

However, Kate knew me better. She rang me at the week-end and told me she thought I would need to rest my swallowing for some time. When I asked her how long, she replied, 'Until I come back from leave.' It was hard to take in what she had said, and knowing Kate as I do I knew she would find it hard as well. Again my emotions were mixed. As she gave me time to talk about it, I felt tearful but could not cry. I just said to her, 'I'll do it but you'll have to cope with the tears.' She suggested that if I was well enough we could meet at the hospital to discuss the matter further. I was very pleased about this because the idea had time to sink in.

When we met, we talked about how I could keep my mouth moist by using a mouth spray. We also discussed communion and how I would manage. Of course, she said I could take communion as long as it was literally only a drop. She emphasised that whilst she didn't want to interfere with something that was so important to me, she had to point out the potential hazards involved. I must admit, her advice made it easier for me to make sure that people only gave me a small amount of the communion wine.

Kate encouraged me to have a weep, to get rid of some of the tension, but I was still too tense. We hugged and said goodbye for a while. She said I could pop in the day she came back. That was something to look forward to. I have always respected her as a professional person, but there is a friendship side to our relationship that means a great deal to me.

Kate arranged for one of her colleagues to keep an eye on me while she was away. This was helpful, because I needed some support to carry out her instructions. We did some work with my tongue to preserve the little movement that remained. She left before Kate came back, but said it had been good to work with me and that she had learned a lot from me. She was different from Kate but a good speech therapist.

I can honestly say I did not have anything orally throughout the appointed time. One or two people suggested I had a go. No one would know. But I was worried about getting another infection and although Kate was far away, I knew she would not suggest such a drastic measure without good reason. Even my GP at the time said she would not interfere. I knew she had not forgotten as she mentioned in a letter that she hoped this hard time was going by quickly and that I was enjoying other things at college.

When Kate returned, I was pleased to see her but I knew I would have to wait before trying to swallow again. The period had been hard and the temptation sometimes great but at least I had made it and my chest was much better.

However, I am not perfect and one day I was absolutely dying for a chocolate button and decided I would try one. I managed to swallow it, but felt so guilty afterwards as I had tried without permission. The next time I saw Kate I confessed and with a twinkle in her eye she said, 'I forgive you.' Knowing what I'm like when I feel guilty she joked with me to put me at ease, but she was pleased I had been able to swallow the button safely and said I could have one a day. She also knows I would have admitted if it had gone wrong. This was the beginning of my being able to take one or two things by mouth under supervision. The next step was two teaspoonsful of yoghurt for tea each day. Then we slowly upgraded the amount. In all, I did not have anything orally for five months and it was another three before I could attempt to swallow food without permission.

I think it is important to tell this story because people do not really understand how dangerous it can be when things 'go down the wrong way'. In some cases it could literally be a matter of life or death. As a result of that episode, if I get a cold or cough I just stop taking anything orally while it lasts. After recovery I build up oral feeding slowly because the cough may linger, and after my experience of pneumonia it is just not worth taking the risk again. So some good did come out of a rotten situation.

Receiving Communion

Due to my swallowing problem, it became difficult for me to receive communion. It became harder for me to take communion in the form of the Host (a small wafer) and at that time in most Catholic churches communion was only given in that one form. I knew it would be possible to receive the Precious Blood in the form of wine as the priests do, but I was unsure how to go about it. I discovered I needed the blessing of the bishop. Bishop David Constance was coming to our parish and the parish priest suggested I had a chat with him.

Father Patrick Purnell and Father Garvey, who knew me well, had already spoken with the bishop so that when I went to see him it was like talking to a friend. He asked me what I wanted the priest to do. I explained to him that I would like to give the priest my spoon so that he could give me the Precious Blood from the spoon. He was happy about this and said he would send me a letter so that I could take it with me wherever I went.

I remember when I was in hospital having the gastrostomy formed, the hospital chaplain was also responsible for the physically disabled in the diocese. I had just lost the ability to drink and had managed to get authorisation to have the Precious Blood. The priest said to me, 'Do you ever think the day will come when you can take the Host?' It took me all my time not to blow my top, and keep calm! He obviously had no idea what I was going through. At that time I was lucky if I could get down a mouthful of tea!

The arrangement worked well for a time, and then I began going to our local parish church and had to explain my situation all over again. The parish priest could not understand why I could not swallow the Host. He also had great difficulty in understanding me, so I had to get somebody to explain on my behalf. By the time that problem was sorted out, the Church began to have ministers for communion so I didn't know who was going to be giving out communion. Fortunately communion in both forms was available. I did have a difficulty in conveying to people that I could not use the spoon myself. In the end I took a card with me to say 'Please help me by taking this spoon from me and giving me the Precious Blood', but this didn't alter the fact that there were always different people, and they did not always understand the situation. I then learned the trick of sitting with somebody I knew who could help me with communion.

This was all very distracting when I was trying to think about what I was doing in receiving the Lord, but I had to try to turn all frustrations about people not knowing what to do into prayer. The parish priest knows me better now and he is more conscious that I have to have communion in this way.

I do not know whether my swallowing ability will worsen, because it is so unpredictable. I have one consolation though. If the worst comes to the worst, I know I could receive communion by the gastrostomy tube. I think we have to remember that, as long as everybody is reverent and sensitive to the situation and behaves with respect, we should not worry. I mention this because there are people who may have to receive communion this way. It is their right.

Reflection

There are a range of reasons why a person may receive nourishment by artificial means. Those who have swallowing problems may include people who have had strokes or head injuries, and many do improve as a result of treatment.

Alternative feeding via a nasogastric tube or gastrostomy may be undertaken as a temporary measure, but some may need a permanent non-oral method of feeding. This does not necessarily mean that nothing can be taken by mouth. Some people use a gastrostomy as a means of 'top-up'. For example, they may be able to eat a small meal and receive the rest in fluid form by tube. Others may need most of their food by tube and just eat a little for pleasure. I have six cans of liquid feed a day and some days I try to take a little solid food as I have described.

Taking a meal features high as a social event, so it is important for disabled persons to have the opportunity to participate while knowing that whatever their particular problem, adequate nutrition can be accomplished by means appropriate to their individual situation.

12

Getting on with Living

Life Outside the Flat

I have a life outside the flat, like being a member of the
parish. When I first moved, I tried to set up a group for
disabled people in the parish, but it did not work out. Looking
back, I think it was hard for a parish priest to have a disabled
person suggesting something to him, so I let that go. I
continued to go to the Carmelite parish, but in time it seemed
more sensible to try to go to my local parish. I had to educate
them about my problems in receiving communion. Eventually
we got around it. One day somebody invited me to go to the
parish social club, and offered to get me a drink of orange! I
felt a bit insulted but accepted. A friend of mine came along
and said, 'What's the matter, Liz? Have you given up drinking?' She knew perfectly well I hadn't and went and bought
me a glass of sherry. The other people who had given me the
orange said, 'Sorry, Liz. We didn't think you'd be allowed to
drink.'

I like to go to Mass on Saturday night. For a long time I
made my own way there, and then met a member of the
parish called John, who was a local headmaster, and he said
he would come and give me a lift if I wanted to go. We get
on very well. When I was at Heythrop College doing pastoral

theology, he used to tease me about getting my work in on time. Pauline, his wife, and he have always been great friends of mine. Peggy is another member of the parish. She had a disabled child who died a few years ago. Now and again she gives me a lift to Mass and we've got to know each other. She now comes to do voluntary work for me on a Monday night, mainly odd jobs around the house and occasionally she may do some typing. Like me, she likes computers.

Another member of the parish is called Vanessa. She is a teacher in the local school. She often picks me up on a Sunday if I want to go to Mass. I have got to know her family quite well, especially William, her son. He often does odd jobs for me, like giving me a lift or taking me shopping. Vanessa likes computers too and she tries to learn more. Now and again it's nice because I have been able to help her solve a problem on her computer. If I get stuck and need a bit of help, I know I could always ring Vanessa or Peggy, but I have this arrangement that they must say no if they can't come. This way it doesn't put a strain on our friendship, and now and again we check it out. Maybe they got to know me because I am disabled, but our friendship goes far beyond that now. We have a lot of fun as well as discussing serious topics.

The Little Sisters of Jesus live across the road about a two-minute walk away from me, and I often pop in to see them. They have a little chapel and sometimes I go there and pray and reflect on life. They always seem to have children among them, and I have got to know some of them. It's nice to have contact with children. Sometimes when they have Mass in the chapel, the children serve, and when we talk after the Gospel it's a tonic.

The children bring me right down to earth. One of them asked the priest, 'Did Judas go to heaven?' I cannot remember what was said in answer to this, but the way the question was asked will always stay in my mind! One of the lads is called Johnny and he's about six. One day I was talking to him and he said, 'Liz, if you put your amplifier on I might be able to hear you!' I remember laughing and he said, 'I can hear you when you laugh!'

The children around the estate have got to know me over the years. They often ask me, 'Why do you walk funny?' I try to tell them, and in the process of trying to tell them, the next question is, 'Why do you talk funny?' I try to explain that I was born like this and that it could have happened to any of their friends. Now and again they call out to me, 'Hello, Liz. How are you?' Sometimes they can't hear me and then they say, 'Can't you talk today?' When it's really a bad day I must confess that I try to avoid them because I do not have the energy to talk to them.

A few years ago I was really 'taken in'. I was walking along to the shop and two girls came towards me. One of them really did look as though she had cerebral palsy. The other girl told me that she couldn't talk and she had nowhere to go in the holidays. I immediately thought of the Have-A-Go Club and thought it might be helpful if she came along. I suggested to the girls that I went to see their parents to talk about the club. As soon as I said that, one of them said, 'Mum's not in.' Then she turned to her friend and said, 'Let's go and get something to eat.' I turned my back, and the minute I did that I could hear them laughing. I looked round again and the girl I thought was disabled was walking perfectly down the road and talking to her sister. I felt such an idiot. I had never in my life been 'taken in' so well. I was annoyed for a few minutes but then I thought, 'Kids!', and saw the funny side of it. However, I'm sure if that had happened to me in my teens I would have thought differently.

About a year before I had my gastrostomy, I needed help

with my supper at the weekends. In our parish we have an organisation called the Society of Vincent de Paul and we asked if anyone could help me. A man called Graham, who is married with three children, agreed to come and help me on Saturdays and Sundays. Initially I wondered how this arrangement would work out, but Graham has been very faithful. He has been coming to me for nine years and he gives me a little solid food if I am feeling up to it.

I think he enjoys coming. We talk about all sorts of things. He's not in the least bit medical, but he tries to understand what I say with regard to my disability and the problems that arise. Obviously, I only let him feed me orally, but he's quite happy to do the washing up! Sometimes I do manage to swallow a little food but most of it goes into my bib. He always tells me I've done well, even if all the food is in the bib! He just accepts it. Some people say men can't wash up, but he's one of the best washer-uppers I know. We've had some great fun over the years when we've been discussing various topics, and sometimes I have to take it all with a pinch of salt. I know his wife, Margaret, and have seen his children grow up. They are a lovely family, and I know I can call on Graham at any time I need to. Sometimes he gives me a lift if he's going my way.

I have a great friend called Sue whom I met in 1979 at St Patrick's in Soho, and we normally meet up on Friday nights, unless one of us has another engagement. She works with the homeless, in an organisation called Thames Reach. I admire what she does and we often sit and talk about the homeless. I normally go to St Patrick's on a Friday night because they have the Stations of the Cross, and then I go on to Pimlico where Sue lives. Or if not, she will come to me.

Five years ago I became friends with a chap called Leo. We were both involved in the Movement for Faith and Light which is an organisation for people with learning difficulties. For a short time we had a group in Tooting. Leo lived just around the corner from me so over the years I had got to know his family as well. The family has a dog and I am always teasing Leo's brother Mark about taking care of it. Sometimes they have parties and I am invited.

Some time ago, Leo moved away to do a course in social work and I do not now see him as much. However, when he does come home, he always pops in to see me and we try to put the world to rights. Not only do we try and sort out our own lives but also those of our friends, and we have long debates about the church. What I value so much about Leo is that he knows I'm disabled and knows what I can and what I cannot do, but that's way down the list of priorities in our friendship. Leo and I are very good friends, and his friendship is something that I shall always value.

About four years ago, Bishop John Crowley invited a group of us to go to Germany. Leo came too. There were about ten of us in the group, including the bishop's secretary, Frances. We went to Germany specifically to have a Bible week and it was great. We had about three sessions a day in which we shared passages from the Bible. Sometimes we did some drawing or acted it out. Once we made up our own psalm and we took the opportunity of celebrating the Eucharist each day. We also took turns to cook, and I helped lay the table when I could. Leo and Frances would sometimes take me for a walk in my wheelchair. This was always great fun. One day we went into a shop to buy some boots for £15 for me. I was so pleased with them that I went back and got another pair.

On the day we were leaving it was my birthday, so we had a celebration at breakfast. That week one of our main texts was from Habakkuk 3:

'Though the fig-tree does not bud and there are no grapes on the vines, though the olive crop fails and the fields produce no food, though there are no sheep in the pen and no cattle in the stalls, yet I will rejoice in the Lord, I will be joyful in God my Saviour.' (NIV)

For my birthday present they gave me a framed copy of this text which I now keep on my wall at home. It will always remind me of Annette who was the leader of the group. I was glad to have the opportunity to make the trip and Bishop John and I have remained good friends.

An Unexpected Letter

My mother and brother, Paul, came to collect me on my return journey from seeing the Pope in Rome. We arrived back in the flat about 9.30 p.m. My mother does not normally interfere with my post but on this occasion she did. On Her Majesty's Service! 'This looks important.' Thinking it was something to do with the social security, I did not take much notice but she read it before I did. 'Congratulations, darling!' I hadn't a clue what she was talking about. All I could see was the happiness on my mother's face. The letter was from Downing Street telling me that I had been awarded the British Empire Medal for the work I had done with the Have-A-Go holiday project, though I did not know this until later. All I could take in was my mother's happiness. Although she does not say much I could read her face.

Father was not there but I felt he should know immediately. I telephoned. 'Father, I have something important to tell you.' 'I know,' he replied, 'you saw the Pope.' I told him that I had seen the Pope not once but twice and that I had given him a copy of my book, but that there was something more I had to say. I told him the secret and he was thrilled.

The announcement would be made on 14th June, the Queen's official birthday. The hardest thing was keeping the news to myself till then. I remember getting up on that day and going straight round to the newsagent to buy my paper so that I could see the announcement in print. I brought the paper back, and it took me ages to find my name among the many others on the Honours List. Very soon people were congratulating me, and then I knew it was true. Jackie, who set the project up, and ILEA sent me cards.

The day after I heard, my parents arranged for me to have a party at home to celebrate with my family. Not all the family knew what it was all about till my father told them. They were pleased for me. I can remember it was a lovely sunny day and we sat out in the garden. It is a day I will always remember with the family.

I heard that the day for the investiture would be 26th November, and that I could take four guests to the ceremony. There were my parents, of course, but it was very difficult to choose two others, so many people had encouraged me. I decided to take my friend, Teresa, who had helped me with my first book and Kate, my speech therapist.

I had great fun deciding what to wear. My parents took me out and bought me a dress and some posh shoes. On the day I had my hair done in the morning. As Donna (from community care) was helping me to dress, she asked if I had a camera. I told her that my camera was broken and I was sure Father would forget to bring his, so she ran home to get hers. My parents arrived. We picked up Kate and then we went to County Hall.

I had been to County Hall many times but never into the Grand Room. The stewards said that one person could sit with me. Dilemma! If my mother came then my father should come too, so I asked Kate. We all sat there very nervously, not knowing what to say to each other. We had the medal and the dissertation (recommendation) in front of us. I could hardly believe what it said. It brought back so many memories.

At about 2.30 p.m. the platform party arrived. The medals were to be presented by the Lord Lieutenant of Greater London, Marshal Sir Edwin Bramail. He spoke to each person and he asked me if any of the people I had helped were there today. I said 'No', but that they knew I was coming. I was worried about standing up although Kate was supporting me from behind. He could not pin the medal on my dress, so I asked Kate to do that.

Afterwards we had tea in one of the main halls. We all had our own table, and sandwiches and cake were provided. I knew I could not eat either of these foods but prior to the day we had contacted the caterers and told them I could eat meringues. Meringues appeared! I had one and my visitors demolished the rest! This was the first time I had eaten in public since my problems with swallowing had developed. I wore a bib but nobody seemed to mind.

From there we went to St Patrick's, Soho, where Father Garvey said the 6 p.m. Mass for me. We had a party afterwards to which all my family came and many of my friends. I was a little sad that I could not invite some of my disabled friends but there were insurmountable stairs – much too difficult a climb for those who are disabled.

The reason I recount this episode at length is not for people to give me a pat on the back, although, being human, that's not to say I didn't enjoy people congratulating me. The main reason is to show what disabled people can give to society. They can do good for others just as much as able-bodied people, if they are given the opportunity and the motivation. If I can do it and have it recognised, then so can other disabled people contribute to society as well if not better than I have done.

There was another exciting event that happened in 1986. I had the opportunity to go to Rome with Across. We stayed in a convent and on the Wednesday morning we went down to St Peter's Square to the audience with the Pope. He walked around, and I gave him a copy of my first book, *Disabled but I Trust*. It was a great privilege to be so near him. We were fortunate to be in Rome for Pentecost Sunday and on the Saturday evening, the eve of Pentecost, we celebrated Pentecost in St Peter's. The Pope presided. Again he walked around among the people and he was very near me. I think that celebration of Pentecost was one of the best ever for me. We were celebrating the feast of Pentecost, commemorating the coming of the Holy Spirit to the apostles. There was a great atmosphere of joy and peace that I have not experienced anywhere else. When we celebrate the feast of Pentecost my mind always goes back to when I was in Rome.

Westminster Missionaries

In 1981, I got to know the organisation called the Westminster Missionaries. This is an organisation mainly for young people who have left school and want more support regarding their faith whilst doing further studies or starting work. In some areas of London people form groups where they can meet together and share their problems regarding work, faith and ideas. As time went on the movement took on more of an ecumenical slant. We have three groups who live as a community and sometimes other members come to join in a community evening.

Over the last three years the movement has spread as far as Edinburgh, Derby and one or two other places besides London. If people wish, we try to find them a spiritual companion to help them on their journey. One of the aspects the movement has taken on is an interest in the Third World and recycled goods, trying not to buy goods that exploit the people of the Third World. So we keep reminding each other to be careful what we buy.

For the past two years I have been on the management committee and I have also been involved in editing a magazine, *Oasis*, which I enjoy doing very much. It is good for me because the organisation is something completely outside the disabled world but at the same time it is interested in matters that concern disability. Another thing that attracted me to the organisation is the fact that it has become ecumenical, which I think is very important in the Christian way of life.

The group which I attend is the West London group. We meet each month and take it in turns to lead a discussion on different issues. My time for serving on the management committee is nearly over. I have mixed feelings about this as I know I shall miss it. However, I have agreed to sit on the fund-raising committee instead, so I will still be keeping in touch with what is going on.

Talks

I have regularly been asked to give talks to various groups. This is a real challenge. Naturally, when I am not having severe speech problems, I have a fairly soft voice which I find very hard to project. I suck ice or put an ice-pack round my throat immediately before speaking. Alcohol also, I am not ashamed to say, helps relax my throat. Pressing my hand or a cushion on my diaphragm is beneficial too. If I am going to speak for a long time, I have to pause for longer periods than the average person in order to get my breath and relax my muscles. I need to be well supported and have a place to rest my head. Even before I start to think about the content of what I want to say, I have to make sure of many details as to how I am going to manage physically. One might say it is ridiculous for a person like me to attempt to speak in public but, if people ask you and you feel you have something to say, what can you do? My experiences have been very mixed.

I remember that in 1981 Jean Vanier, the founder of L'Arche, took a pilgrimage of people with learning difficulties to Lourdes. He asked me if I would be prepared to talk to parents. He also asked Mary Craig (who wrote *Blessings* and many other books) and one or two others to talk that same evening. The place was the Upper Basilica and about four hundred parents were present. On hearing this I was flabbergasted. What was I going to say? He wanted me to talk about suffering. I decided to talk about my brother, Vincent, and the struggles he had and how these had affected my parents and me. I remember saying that besides knowing the pains and joys of being disabled myself, I could also understand something of what my parents must have suffered and sympathise with them. I was aware that I could not take their sadness away. I also said that my parents' experience was different from my own.

That evening it was more important that people should hear what I had to say than they should become conscious of the effort I had to make to speak. Therefore, I asked an old friend of mine, Teresa de Bertadano, to stand by me and translate. I would say a few sentences and she would repeat it to the audience. At the end they applauded and although I was very tired and wanted to go to bed, people continued to ask questions. I said I would see them the next day and asked the lady who was pushing my chair to take me back to my hotel. A few parents came to continue the dialogue the morning afterwards.

The next big talk I gave was at Worth Abbey. Dr Therese Vanier asked me if I would join her in talking about suffering and compassion. Therese was a cancer specialist. We followed the same pattern as in Lourdes. Having someone repeat what I was saying enabled me to get my breath between sentences as well as making it possible for all to hear. There were about four hundred young people in the audience. I spoke about how different people in my life had shown me compassion as my disabilities increased, especially those of swallowing and incontinence. These were people who did not duck the real issues; they did not pretend that they had any easy answers when none existed. This was real compassion. Unless you have some understanding of suffering you won't have much compassion. I think compassion is a gift which comes our way as we suffer. I cannot tell what effect I had on those young people. What I wanted to convey was that God's love is present in suffering and in a mysterious way God communicates his love through the pain.

Paul Fagin persuaded me to speak at an event organised by CAFOD at Wembley Conference Centre. I thought I was to speak to a small group of about forty people; the small group turned out to be six hundred. Paul came to my flat with a video to demonstrate what was going to happen. I was one of a number of speakers, including a black person, somebody who was homeless and somebody unemployed. Paul himself suffers from spina bifida but, apart from a limp, you would not know it.

Therese Vanier came again and acted as my 'voice'. This time in order to help myself relax I sucked ice. Tactfully and lovingly Therese explained to the audience what would happen. They had to get me on to the stage and Paul made a song and dance about that, complaining how difficult disabled people were and what a burden they were on society, just to demonstrate to the audience how society does in fact treat disabled people.

It was a nerve-racking experience but my friends, Sister Madeleine Prendergast and Father Patrick Purnell, were there to support me. Patrick gave me confidence because he knew what was going on inside me and so I focused my eyes on him. I spoke about my disability – the suffering and joy of it – and about the holiday project. When it came to questions, a lady in the audience, whom I did not know, asked me if I ever felt that it would have been a better thing if I had been aborted. I cannot remember exactly what I said in reply, but I told her that I would not change my life for anything. I will never forget that occasion. Undoubtedly, life has been difficult but disability has provided me with so many challenges to overcome and win through.

The next talk I gave was at Wormwood Scrubs Prison. Three hours before I was due to speak I still had not prepared. I had been to my doctor and we had had an argument over my gastrostomy tubes. I told her about the talk and she said, 'Good, it will take your mind off yourself!' She told me later that she did not know what to do with me at that moment, so ended up telling me I was making a fuss about nothing. She actually was an excellent GP, but on that occasion she really upset me and I needed to ring Father Garvey to help me calm down. He was just intrigued by what I was going to do, which put things into proportion and I felt ready to go ahead.

It wasn't until I eventually got through the security systems and into Wormwood Scrubs that I really relaxed. I talked about what it was like to be disabled, what I had managed to achieve and how my faith had helped me. I said I was trapped in a body which would not do what I wanted it to do and compared my experience to that of being locked in a cell and not being able to get out.

It was a very moving experience. I gained so much from meeting the inmates, much more than they could ever have gained from me. When it came to questions, one man asked me whether I was bitter because I was disabled. I remember thinking and answering that I hoped I was not. I found it difficult to say exactly where I was on the issue of bitterness. It was sometimes hard not to be but deep down I didn't think I really knew what bitterness was. It was hard to give a direct answer. I was pleased to hear that the men felt very positive about what I had said and I hope one day I will have the opportunity to return there. At that time one of the Birmingham Six was in the Scrubs. I just wonder how many other innocent people were there!

Reflection

I have a number of activities outside the flat. When you live on your own this is very important regardless of whether you are disabled or not. This is why I try to have outside interests and become involved in others' concerns that have nothing to do with disability. Yes, I am disabled but I am also a human being and need contact with other fellow human beings. It is very important to keep the balance right. That way, one can see life in proportion. At least, that's the way I see it.

13

The Last Year

My Family

The last year has been full of exciting events as well as some disappointments. My nephews and nieces, nine boys and five girls, are all getting on well at school and the two eldest are studying for GCSE. Two of my nephews are into sport in a big way, and one or two of them are keen on music which pleases my father no end. The older ones are forming relationships and we had great fun at Christmas teasing them about it. My sister's two adopted children seem to be settling down very well and enjoy seeing their grandparents.

I do not see much of my nephews and nieces, except on family occasions. I would love to be able to invite them to visit me or to go out with them, and I do hope that as they grow older this may be possible. Because they do not see me very often it takes a long time for me to build relationships with them, and it does sadden me that they only see me as their aunt who is disabled. However, the older ones do chat to me on the phone when I ring their parents, so I am sure we will get to know each other better as time goes by. The older ones also know that I am writing this book and when we talk they enquire what I have written and whether it is hard to write a book. It has become a topic of conversation so I feel very encouraged by their interest.

Early last year my mother became unwell. It is very difficult to identify the exact problem. For a number of years my mother has been finding it hard to keep her balance. Early in the year she began getting shaking attacks and when this was happening she gave the impression of being unconscious – but she was not. She would go to sleep and then wake up and carry on. She went into hospital for investigations to try to get to the root of the problem. This proved to be very difficult but the doctors did manage to prescribe some medication that would help control the situation.

In the meantime, my mother had deteriorated physically and at times became very confused. She now finds it difficult to walk and has to use a wheelchair outside the flat. My father has to help her to dress and to feed herself. This is very hard on both of them because their roles have been reversed. My father is nearly eighty and my mother almost seventy-nine, so as much as Father wants to look after Mother, it is a very difficult and painful situation but they manage very well.

Some while back I was visiting my parents. My father was busy cooking the lunch and my mother was struggling to dress. I said I would see if I could give her a hand. I did manage to help her to put her socks on, although it was a bit like the blind leading the blind. My mind went back to all the times my mother had helped me with everyday things that other people take for granted and how much care she has given me over the years. She would always help me on with my coat when I was leaving to return to the flat. Even now, on a good day she will try and get up to help me put my coat on, but of course it is very difficult for her, but it is nice to know she still wants to do it.

I find it very hard indeed because I used to depend on my

mother for little things that had I not been disabled I would not have needed. Harder and more painful to bear is the knowledge that I would like to be able to look after my mother. I am single and have no ties. I would gladly be at home helping my parents. This, however, is impossible, given my situation.

I used to talk at length with my mother about politics and debate with her about the Church. I miss being able to 'wind up' my mother in a good conversation. It is very difficult now to communicate with my mother – not because of my speech defects but because Mother gets confused by what is being said to her. It is no longer possible to talk with her as we used to.

As a family we are all finding it very hard to deal with this new scenario and we try to support each other. I must admit I often have a weep about it, while making sure I keep this from the rest of the family. My heart goes out to my father because sometimes my mother is not sure who he is and that is very, very painful for him. There is little one can do to help. I try to support by listening; by making sure that he does get help with giving the physical care that my mother now needs; and also by ensuring that he gets some respite to refuel his batteries. The kind of caring for a loved one that he is giving is so tiring, but we know Father would not want it any other way as long as he is able to manage.

Recently, my mother had a fall and had to return again to hospital. Mother had a rough time and my father had always felt that the drugs she was taking were not quite right. He managed to see the consultant and with time the hospital was able to get the medication right. Mother has now returned home and is coping with life much better. She still needs the wheelchair, but sometimes likes a little walk. My parents have help on the weekdays, and the rest of the time my father looks after her, although she can do a little more for herself at the moment. It is nice to be able to chat to Mother again, and although she is a little deaf which makes things harder, we laugh and get by.

The rest of the family pop in when they can. Mary likes to help around the house. Felicity and Paul take my parents out and I go and keep them company each week. So at the moment things are easier. As my mother often says, 'Just take one day at a time.' I have talked about Mother, but my father has been great through my mother's illness. It is touching to see them coping with it together.

Holiday in Portugal

My sister Mary's son belongs to a rugby club. Mary was selling some raffle tickets for the club, and being a good sister I bought a book of these. Surprise, surprise when I won the main prize! It was a trip to the Algarve, Portgual. I could take three people with me to share a villa for a week. I had great fun deciding who to ask. I wanted to take people who knew me more as a person than somebody who was disabled. I dropped hints to one or two people and they only sounded half-interested. So I thought a bit harder and longer and I thought I would ask two men friends – Leo and William whom I have mentioned previously. I also thought that would get everybody talking, which was really what I wanted to do!

I had already been to Lourdes a number of times with a friend called Joan who happened to be a nurse. I can honestly say I get on well with her so I asked her if she would like to come. In principle everyone agreed. It was just a question of getting the dates sorted out. This did not present much of a difficulty so on an October morning we set out for Portugal.

I was really looking forward to the trip but I was a bit concerned as to whether everyone would get on with each other. We had a supper at my flat to all meet together. That seemed to go well. I went to stay with Joan the night before we travelled and Joan's friend, David, drove us to the airport. It was about 5 a.m. Inside, I was worried whether the lads would get up and turn up in time for the flight. Of course they did, though they did look half-asleep – a reflection of the way we were all feeling. The journey was pleasant and it gave Leo and William a chance to get to know each other. Joan and I were lucky, we could have a sleep during the flight.

When we arrived, the boys went off to get the hire car and we had great fun trying to get all our luggage on to the roof rack and ourselves into the car. Eventually the lads made a good job of stowing the bags and we were off. We had even more fun trying to read the map to find our way. It felt rather as if we had been all round the world but eventually we arrived at our villa. We had a snack to eat and then all collapsed and went to sleep.

I did not want to appear bossy but there was a loose rug on the floor and I said straight away that it was coming up – because I knew I would have fallen over it before long. That would have made more work for my friends. I was a bit concerned because Joan had a cold and did not seem at all well. So I told her to stay in bed that night – I have never known Joan allow anyone to tell her what to do before! I'm glad I did because she was much better the next day.

The boys and I went out to have a meal and a look round the town. The next day we all went out to explore and took the car with us and my wheelchair so that we could walk further. We all went to Mass on the Sunday and it was all in Portuguese. I did not understand much of what was being said. Leo luckily had a phrase book and managed to convey my communion needs to the priest and ensured that I had communion. Leo and I went to Mass twice more that week. By the end of the week we were well-known to the parish. One lady asked Leo if I was his mother! I don't know who was the most put out – him or me. I often tease him about this when I want to put him in his place.

We organised things so that the boys did the shopping and they were good at this. We made sightseeing trips and spent time on the beach when I was able to go into the sea. I did enjoy that because I had not been in the sea for a long, long time. I could only get Joan to wet her feet, but she was very good about helping me to get dried and dressed when I came out.

We usually had our evening meal out in a different restaurant each evening. I had a feed before we went out, and had a go at trying to eat a little food orally. My friends were very sensitive about that. We seemed to have a lot of stimulating conversations – politics, nursing, child care – and I dare say I got in my bit about disability. It was great fun. I really enjoyed myself. The week just flew by. Before we knew it, it was time to fly home. Unfortunately, there was a delay so we had a long wait at the airport, but we made the best of it by sitting in the sunshine. We arrived back in London about 6 p.m., some four hours later than anticipated, all very tired but happy.

I could only say it was one of the best holidays I have ever had. I think it was partly because I felt free and accepted for who I am.

Studies

I am planning to do an Open University foundation course in Society and Social Science. The course promises to be very interesting and stimulating, and I am sure it will broaden my outlook on life and society. The radio and television will become important to me because, along with reading, these will provide the main means of accessing course material for study. I also have to produce a series of essays for assessment purposes to a fairly tight schedule of deadlines, so I will really have to discipline myself. I did an Open University course in 1975 so I know what I am in for.

Work for the Future

Currently I am a member of the Community Health Council (CHC) for my area. The CHC is an independent body set up to monitor the National Health Service (NHS) and ensure that the interests of local people are taken into account. The skills needed to be an effective CHC member are an ability to look at services from the perspective of clients and carers, to listen to the views of individuals from different parts of the community, and to assist in representing those views to those who plan and manage health services.

I find this a very interesting and challenging responsibility because every aspect of health care is involved, not just disability. The experience is good for me personally because I have become involved and concerned with the community of which I am part. I am also increasingly aware that my presence on the CHC is valued by my fellow members. In spite of my communication difficulties, my contribution is always encouraged and I am always given time to make my point. The most gratifying aspect is that some of my ideas or suggestions have been taken into consideration.

CHC members are accorded access to all parts of the NHS. When we visit hospital wards or departments, it is fully accepted that I will do so in my wheelchair. Of course this means I am in a unique position to examine certain aspects of the service from the consumer point of view!

In the near future I am hoping to write a small pamphlet on the sacraments in relation to disabled people. When I was at Heythrop College I wrote a dissertation which contained a section on the sacraments. I am hoping I can revise and expand this so that it can be of help to others. Disabled people can feel very powerless, but they can also be very powerful. This is another aspect of life I would like to explore and write about.

At the end of each year I renew my commitment, and I ask myself what I am doing for my fellow disabled people. I try to support them on committees, by speaking up for them, and for people who work for them. However, I will not participate in violence or demonstrations which discredit the disabled group in the eyes of the public at large. I feel disquiet when such events are portrayed in the media, though I do appreciate that some individuals feel that this is the way to make their point. I feel that by writing, prayer and reflection I may reach out to more people, on behalf of the people who are disabled.

Final Reflection

Much time was spent pondering a title for this book, not just by myself but also by my friend, Joan, who has helped me in the later stages. However, neither of us won that particular battle. It was a child named Jenny, aged thirteen, who looked at the chapter contents list and out of the blue said 'Life, the unclear path', which quickly became *The Unclear Path* because that is life for any of us – unclear.

This leads me to the issue of my responses when people ask me if my disability will worsen. If I am honest, this is a question that is always at the back of my mind. Nobody knows the answer, but one thing I know is that I will strive to make the best of life by both giving and receiving.

In the introduction to this book I mentioned that my faith is very important to me, and that the love of God can work and spread through other people whether they are aware of this or not. God's love is much deeper than words can express. Sometimes when I am attempting to pray or attending Mass, like many other people, I find that God seems far away. It seems important to give time to prayer. There would be something missing from life if I did not. I may wake during the night and, without thinking about it, prayer and praise enter my head. But the prayer itself may seem desolate. However, there is this impulse within me at gut-level to carry on trying to pray regardless. I am aware that God does answer my prayer but it may not be in the way I expect. We are told to ask for what we need and I do ask for my needs and the needs of the world, but asking is not the essence of my prayer. The real core of prayer is praise and thanksgiving.

I am often distracted when I pray, but over the years I have come to understand that distractions are part of praying. I have had to learn how to treat them as prayer and not to worry about them. If distractions could not be turned into prayer, I think I would have given up trying to pray long ago. Patrick will be thinking, 'At long last, some of what I have said to her no end of times has sunk in.' He has also helped me to see prayer as a gift which I hope I will never lose. It is equally important to add that there are times when I experience great joy and peace in prayer, and the presence of God is very near. This I hang on to particularly at times when God can seem distant, but of course He is there all the time.

The second point I want to end on is that if I look back on my life so far, I feel very strongly that God has touched me through people. I would identify these people as many: my family, people who have helped me on a professional level, people who have become friends. Some have shown me great compassion and honesty and have helped me as I have struggled through life. The goodness in them cannot necessarily be strictly defined, but the hand of God has touched me through them whether they are aware of it or not. Most of the time I am unaware that it is happening. It is only in retrospect that I realise what has occurred. I am not going to attempt to mention people by name because there would be far too many. However, I do just want to affirm again that it is this that keeps me ticking and struggling on to promote the kingdom of God in whatever way I can.

Throughout my life, I have had many ups and downs and I have had to struggle in many ways. The one thing that keeps me going is that I can look back on life, thus far, and say, 'GOD has never tried me beyond my strength.'